It's another Quality Book from CGP

This book is for anyone doing GCSE Physical Education.

First, we've stuck in all the really important stuff
you need to do well in GCSE PE.

Then we've had a really good stab at making it
slightly entertaining — so you'll actually use it.

Simple as that.

What CGP is all about

Our sole aim here at CGP is to produce the highest quality
books — carefully written, immaculately presented, and
dangerously close to being funny.

Then we work our socks off to get them out to you
— at the cheapest possible prices.

Contents

Section 1 — The Human Body

Bones 1
Joints 2
Muscles 4
The Respiratory System 6
The Circulation 8
Revision Summary 10

Section 2 — Health and Fitness

Health 11
Fitness 12
Exercise 13
The Effects of Exercise 14
Diet and Nutrition 16
Energy 18
Endurance 19
Strength, Speed and Power 20
Flexibility 21
Age and Gender 22
Somatotype 23
Sport and Personality 24
Hygiene 25
Drugs 26
Other Things that Affect Performance 28
Revision Summary 29

Section 3 — Training and Sporting Skills

Training Sessions 30
Training Methods..32
Fitness Testing 34
Sporting Injuries 36
Injuries — Types and Treatment...38
Skills 40
Motivation and Mental Preparation 42
Revision Summary..43

Section 4 — Sport in Society

Leisure and Recreation 44
Participation in Sport 45
Women in Sport 46
Sporting Behaviour 47
Local Sports Clubs 48
Sporting Facilities 49
Sporting Bodies and Organisations 50
Finance of Sport 52
Sponsorship 53
Sport and the Media 54
Amateurs and Professionals 55
International Sport 56
The Olympic Games 57
Revision Summary..58

Index 59

Published by Coordination Group Publications Ltd.

Contributors:
Charley Darbishire
Simon Little
Andy Park
Glenn Rogers

And:
Chris Dennett
Katherine Stewart

ISBN: 978 1 84146 709 2

Groovy website: www.cgpbooks.co.uk
Jolly bits of clipart from CorelDRAW®
Printed by Elanders Hindson Ltd, Newcastle upon Tyne.

Text, design, layout and original illustrations © Coordination Group Publications Ltd. 2000
All rights reserved.

Section One — The Human Body

Bones

The skeleton gives the body its shape and has loads of jobs to do. It's made up of various kinds of bones, all meeting at joints — and different joints move in different ways. Clever stuff.

The Skeleton has Different Functions

The skeleton does a lot more than you might think. Learn what it does and learn the names of the most important bones. The main functions are:

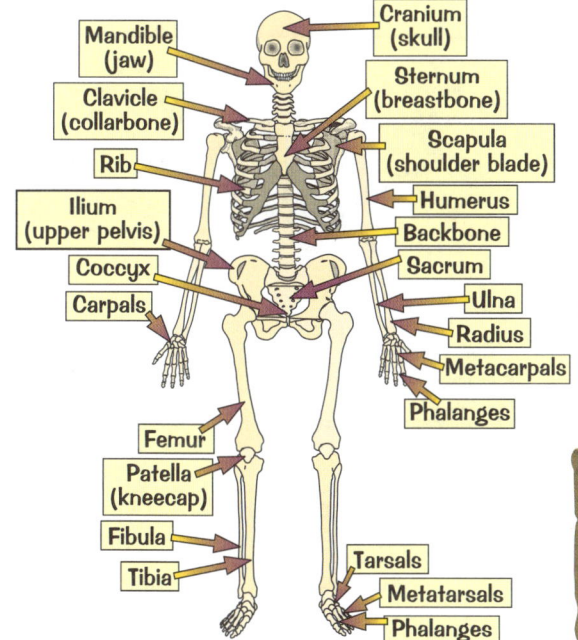

Labelled skeleton diagram: Mandible (jaw), Cranium (skull), Clavicle (collarbone), Sternum (breastbone), Rib, Scapula (shoulder blade), Ilium (upper pelvis), Humerus, Coccyx, Backbone, Carpals, Sacrum, Ulna, Radius, Metacarpals, Phalanges, Femur, Patella (kneecap), Fibula, Tibia, Tarsals, Metatarsals, Phalanges.

① **SUPPORT:**
1) The skeleton is a rigid frame for the rest of the body.
2) The skeleton supports the soft tissues.
3) Without the skeleton, we'd collapse like jelly.

② **SHAPE:**
1) Our shape is mainly due to our skeleton.

An adult human has 206 bones. Exercise and diet are both important in maintaining bone strength throughout life.

③ **PROTECTION:**
1) Bones are very tough.
2) They protect delicate organs — like the brain, heart and lungs.

④ **MOVEMENT:**
1) There are loads of joints.
2) Muscles, attached by tendons, can move various bones.

⑤ **MAKING BLOOD CELLS:**
1) Long bones contain bone marrow.
2) New blood cells are made in this bone marrow.

Bones are Formed by the Ossification of Cartilage

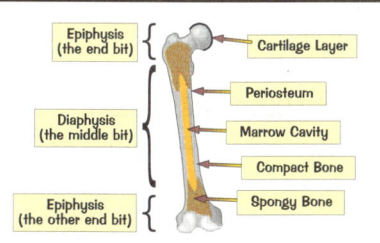

Diagram of long bone: Epiphysis (the end bit), Cartilage Layer, Periosteum, Diaphysis (the middle bit), Marrow Cavity, Compact Bone, Epiphysis (the other end bit), Spongy Bone.

1) All bones start off as cartilage in the womb. They gradually turn to bone by ossification — but it takes years for some bones.
2) Bones have a tough outer layer called the periosteum — except where they've got cartilage instead.
3) Spongy bone is light but tough. Some spongy bone contains red marrow, where red blood cells are made.
4) The marrow cavity contains yellow marrow, where white blood cells form.

There are Four Different Types of Bone

Remember these different types of bone — you'll need to know them for the exam.

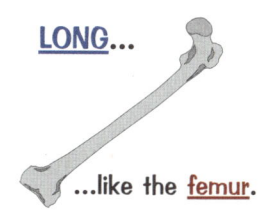

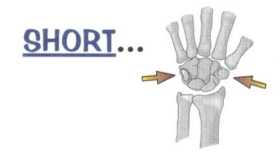

LONG... ...like the femur.

SHORT... ...squarish bones like the carpals (wrist) and tarsals (ankle).

FLAT... ...like some bones in the skull.

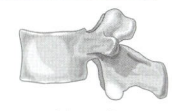

IRREGULAR... ...like the vertebrae.

No bones about it — it's a humerus little page...

The skeleton is dead important. Imagine life without it — we'd all be wobbling about like blancmanges. So you need to know what the skeleton does — and I mean all of it. You should also learn the names of the important bones in the body, and the different types of bones.

Joints

Your backbone is all-important, with all its different sections. And as for all that connective tissue — the string and glue that holds us together — well, maybe you'd better learn about that too...

The Spine has Five Different Sections

The vertebral column (or spine) is divided up into different sections, and each section contains some smallish bones called vertebrae (each one is a 'vertebra').

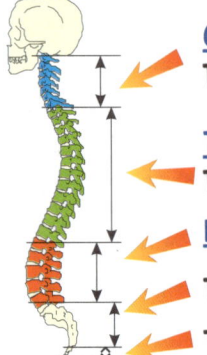

Cervical vertebrae — you have 7 of these. These make up the neck.

Thoracic vertebrae — you have 12 of these. The ribs are attached to these.

Lumbar vertebrae — you have 5 of these.

The sacrum — that's this triangular shaped bone.

The coccyx — it does nothing now, but it used to be a tail.

This is the pelvis, seen from the front.

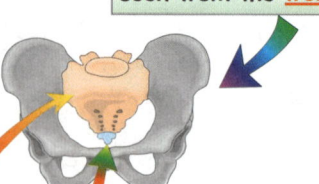

Connective Tissues Join Muscle and Bones

There are three types of connective tissue you need to know about.

CARTILAGE — forms cushions between bones to stop them rubbing.

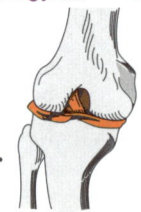

LIGAMENTS — like very strong string that holds bones together.

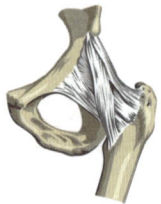

TENDONS — attach muscles to bones (or to other muscles).

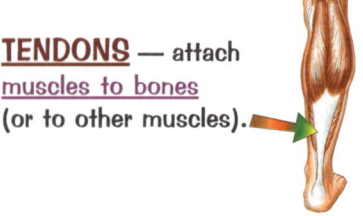

There are Three Different Types of Joint

Not all joints allow movement. There are three different types for you to know about:

1) FIXED, OR IMMOVABLE JOINTS — These are also called fibrous joints.

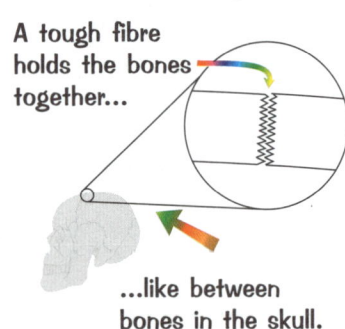

A tough fibre holds the bones together...

...like between bones in the skull.

2) SLIGHTLY MOVABLE JOINTS — These are sometimes called cartilaginous joints.

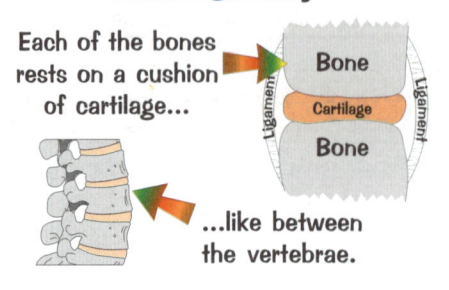

Each of the bones rests on a cushion of cartilage...

...like between the vertebrae.

The bones can move a little bit — but ligaments stop them moving too far...

3) FREELY MOVABLE JOINTS — These are sometimes called synovial joints.

These contain synovial fluid inside a pocket called the synovial membrane...

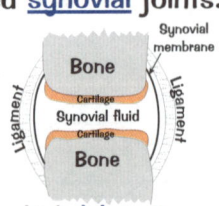

...which lubricates (or 'oils') the joint.

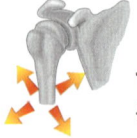

The shoulder joint is a freely movable joint.

All the moving parts are held together by ligaments.

Without vertebrae, we'd all be spineless...

Loads more dead important stuff here. If a page like this looks a bit much, just take it a section at a time. After learning each bit, always make sure you really have learnt it. The best way to do that's just to scribble it all down on a scrap piece of paper — then check back to make sure it's all right.

Section One — The Human Body

Joints

These joints are clever old things — they let bits of your body move in certain directions. You'll need to know the kinds of movement your body can make, and the types of joints.

There are Five Kinds of Joint Movement

There are five different kinds of movement the joints can allow. You need to know the info.

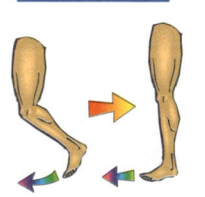

EXTENSION — Opening a joint.

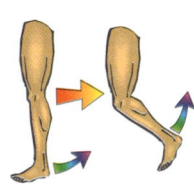

FLEXION — Closing a joint.

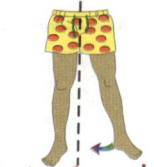

ADDUCTION — Moving towards an imaginary centre line.

ABDUCTION — Moving away from an imaginary centre line.

ROTATION — Turning a limb clockwise or anticlockwise.

There are Five Types of Movable Joint you need to know

Your shoulder can move in more directions than your knee. That's because it's a different kind of joint. Here are the five kinds you'd better learn:

BALL AND SOCKET — like the hip or shoulder.

The joint can move in all directions, and it can rotate as well.

So this allows flexion, extension, adduction, abduction and rotation.

HINGE — like the knee or elbow.

The joint can go backwards and forwards, but not side-to-side.

This allows flexion and extension.

PIVOT — like the joint in your spine that lets you shake your head.

This joint is between the atlas and axis bones in your neck. This kind of joint only allows rotation.

CONDYLOID — like the wrist.

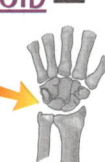

The joint can move forwards and backwards, left to right — but it can't rotate.

Allows flexion, extension, adduction and abduction.

GLIDING — like between the tarsals or carpals.

The bones move a little bit in all directions by sliding over each other.

Your Muscles and Joints act as Levers

Joints multiply either the force of a muscle, or the speed of a movement. When you bend your elbow, your biceps makes a short movement, but your hand makes a larger one — this means your hand moves more quickly.

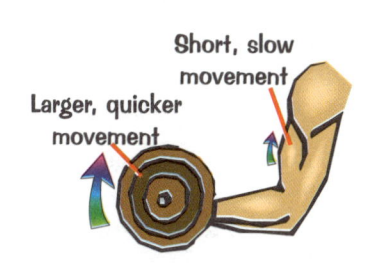

Short, slow movement

Larger, quicker movement

Moving joints — you'd better lever little space...

There's a load of niggly names to learn here, so give it some time. It can be a bit tricky, but try to think of ways to remember things. Like this: ADDuction is bringing two bits together, kind of like 'adding' them — while ABDuction is taking them away — like when you're abducted by aliens.

Section One — The Human Body

Muscles

There's lots to know about the muscle system. You need to know the three different types of muscle, and the names of the bigger, or more important, muscles. Here's everything you need...

There are Three Different Types of Muscle

Like the title says, there are three different types of muscle. These are...

CARDIAC MUSCLES
1) Only in the heart.
2) Contract and relax continuously.
3) Work without conscious effort from you.

INVOLUNTARY MUSCLES
1) Around organs such as the intestines, and blood vessels.
2) Work without conscious effort from you.

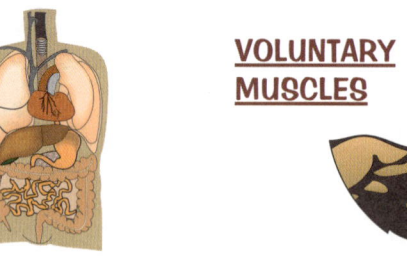

VOLUNTARY MUSCLES
1) Attached to the skeleton.
2) Under your control.

Muscles are Made of Loads of Small Fibres

It's important you know what the big important muscles are called. Learn this diagram well.

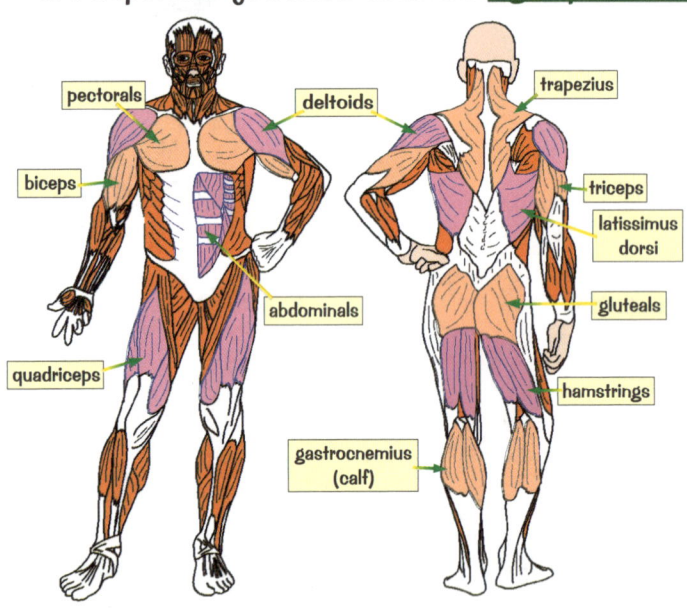

Labels on diagram: pectorals, deltoids, biceps, abdominals, quadriceps, trapezius, triceps, latissimus dorsi, gluteals, hamstrings, gastrocnemius (calf)

1) Muscles are made up of fibres. Only some of these fibres will be ready to do work.
2) All individual voluntary muscle fibres are either fast twitch or slow twitch.
3) Everybody has a similar number of muscle fibres — but different people have different proportions of fast twitch and slow twitch fibres.
4) People who are fit and who have larger muscles have fatter muscle fibres — and more of their fibres are ready to be used.
5) Nerve impulses are what tell muscles to contract (or in the case of the heart, they tell it to speed up or slow down).
6) Complex movements are made possible by the coordination of nerve impulses sent to the muscles by the nervous system.

Fast Twitch for Power, Slow Twitch for Endurance

Fast twitch fibres and slow twitch fibres are good for different things.

Fast twitch fibres contract very quickly and very powerfully — but they get tired quickly.

Top class sprinters and shot-putters have loads of fast twitch fibres.

Fast runner = fast twitch

Slow twitch fibres contract more slowly and with less force — but they don't get tired as quickly.

Top class long distance runners have loads of slow twitch fibres.

Slow runner = slow twitch

Is that a bacon rope I see? No, it's a hamstring...

You should know about the types of muscle in the body, and the names of the bigger voluntary muscles. And make sure you can describe the differences between fast and slow twitch fibres.

Section One — The Human Body

Muscles

You need to know about how muscles work in pairs, and all the fancy names that are used to describe this. You should also learn the effects of exercise and inactivity. All the info's here.

Muscles Pull on Bones

Muscles are attached to two different bones by tendons.
Only one of these bones will move when the muscle contracts.

THE ORIGIN — The place where the muscle's attached to the stationary bone.

THE INSERTION — The place where the muscle's attached to the moving bone.

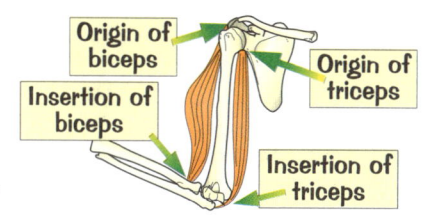

Antagonistic Muscles work in Pairs

Muscles can only do one thing — pull. To make a joint move in two directions, you need two muscles that can pull in opposite directions.

1) Antagonistic muscles are pairs of muscles that work against each other.
2) One muscle contracts (shortens) while the other one relaxes (lengthens) and vice versa.
3) The muscle that's doing the work (contracting) is the prime mover, or agonist.
4) The muscle that's relaxing is the antagonist.
5) There are also muscles called synergists. They hold the stationary bone still, so only one bone moves — e.g. when the bicep contracts to bend the elbow, synergists stop the shoulder moving.

There are Two Types of Muscle Contraction

There are two types of contraction that a muscle can undergo — isometric and isotonic.

ISOMETRIC CONTRACTION
— the muscle stays the same length and so nothing moves.
Like if you pull on a rope attached to a wall.

ISOTONIC CONTRACTION
— the muscle changes length and so something moves.
Like if you exercise with weights that are free to move.

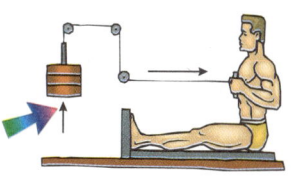

Effects of Using Muscles and Muscle Tone

If you use your muscles constantly, or underuse them, several things can happen.

MUSCLE FATIGUE —
If you use your muscles a lot and they don't get enough oxygen, they feel tired or fatigued.

MUSCLE ATROPHY —
If you don't use your muscles, they get smaller. This is atrophy.

CRAMP —
A sudden contraction of a muscle that won't relax.

Muscles never relax completely — there's always some tension in them. This is called muscle tone. Exercise improves muscle tone, which in turn improves your posture. If you improve your posture, you put less strain on your muscles, joints and bones, and you won't get injured as easily.

You deserve atrophy for learning all this...

'Antagonistic system' sounds pretty gruesome, but it's really quite a simple concept. The trouble is though, you really do need to know the name — oh yes, and all the other stuff on the page too.

Section One — The Human Body

The Respiratory System

The respiratory system is everything we use to breathe and supply our bodies with oxygen. We breathe air into our lungs. The oxygen is then transferred to our blood and taken around our body.

The Air You Breathe Ends Up in the Alveoli

You'll need to know where the air goes on its way to the alveoli.

TRACHEA → **BRONCHI** → **BRONCHIOLES** → **ALVEOLI**

1) Air passes through the nose or mouth and then on to the trachea.

2) The trachea splits into two tubes called bronchi (each one is a 'bronchus') — one going to each lung.

3) The bronchi split into progressively smaller tubes called bronchioles.

4) The bronchioles finally end at small bags called alveoli (each one is an 'alveolus') where the gas exchange takes place.

The area inside the chest containing the lungs, heart and all the other bits is the chest cavity.

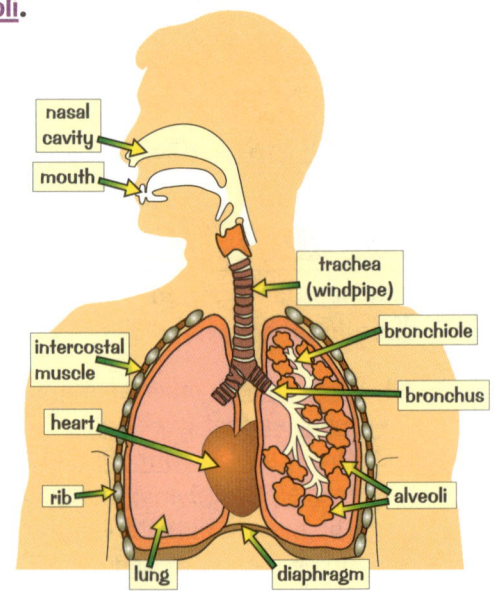

Oxygen and Carbon Dioxide are Exchanged in the Alveoli

There are millions of alveoli in your lungs. This is where the gaseous exchange happens. When you breathe:

1) Carbon dioxide moves from your blood into the alveoli.
2) Oxygen moves across to the red blood cells. The red blood cells contain haemoglobin, which combines with the oxygen to make oxyhaemoglobin.
3) The red blood cells carry the oxygen around the body and deliver it where it's needed. At the same time, the blood collects carbon dioxide to be taken back to the lungs.

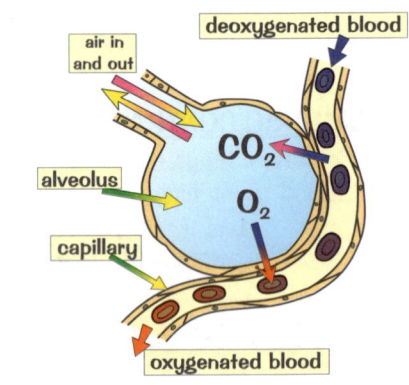

The air you breathe in and the air you breathe out are different. The air you breathe out has less oxygen, because the body's used some — but more carbon dioxide.

	You breathe in...	You breathe out...
Oxygen	21%	17%
Carbon dioxide	Only a tiny wee bit	4%
Water vapour	Not much	Quite a lot
Nitrogen + other inert gases	79%	79%

There is still some oxygen in the air you breathe out — that's why mouth-to-mouth resuscitation works.

Air we go — keeping trachea respiratory system...

This page is OK really — it's just got lots of tricky names that make it seem hard. Cover up the diagrams and quickly sketch them till you know the names. With the table, don't worry too much about the percentages — but do make sure you can explain the differences between the columns.

Section One — The Human Body

The Respiratory System

You'll need to know about how you breathe — and about the ways you can measure the capacity of your lungs. You also need to know how exercise affects your respiratory system.

The Intercostals and Diaphragm Make us Breathe

Breathing in (inspiration):

1) The intercostals and the diaphragm contract to make the chest cavity larger.

2) Air is pushed into the lungs by the air pressure outside.

Breathing out (expiration):

1) The intercostals and the diaphragm relax to make the chest cavity smaller.

2) The lungs are squeezed and air is forced out.

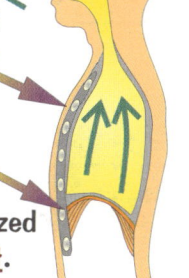

There are Different Types of Lung Capacity

A spirometer measures air breathed in and out, and produces graphs like these. From these graphs you can measure different lung capacities — which can be useful guides to health.

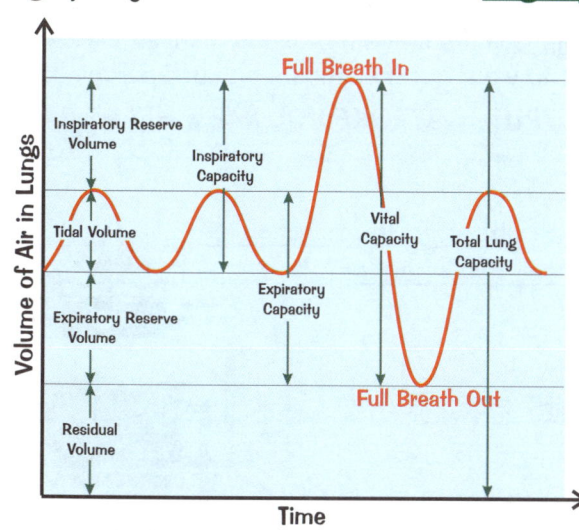

1) **TIDAL VOLUME** is the amount you breathe in (or out) with each breath.

2) **INSPIRATORY CAPACITY** is the most you can breathe in, after breathing out normally.

3) **EXPIRATORY RESERVE VOLUME** is the most air you could force out after breathing out normally.

4) **VITAL CAPACITY** is the most air you could possibly breathe in or out in one breath.

5) **RESIDUAL VOLUME** is the amount of air left in your lungs after you've breathed out as much as possible.

Exercise Increases Your Oxygen Uptake

When you exercise, your body needs more oxygen to make the muscles work. To achieve this:
1) You breathe more quickly.
2) Your heart pumps faster — so the red blood cells travel faster and deliver more oxygen.

That means your oxygen uptake increases. It's measured by your VO_2, which is just the volume of oxygen (O_2) your body uses in a minute.
The maximum it reaches is called your VO_2 Max — the fitter you are, the higher it is.

Take a breather — there's a lung way to go yet...

The way to learn those breathing diagrams is to think about them. Feel yourself breathe in and out and try to relate it to the diagrams. It's the same with the lung capacities — they look hard at first, but give those complicated names a bit of thought and they'll soon make perfect sense...

Section One — The Human Body

The Circulation

Your circulatory system's pretty funky and it's in two bits — they're the pulmonary and systemic circuits. The blood goes round one, then the other, passing through each side of the heart in turn.

The Circulatory System has Three Functions

1) TRANSPORT — moving things around the body in the bloodstream, like oxygen, nutrients (like glucose), water and waste.

2) BODY TEMPERATURE CONTROL — more blood near the skin cools the body quicker. That's why your skin looks redder after exercise.

3) PROTECTION — moving antibodies around the body to fight disease. Blood clotting seals cuts.

Humans have a Double Circulation

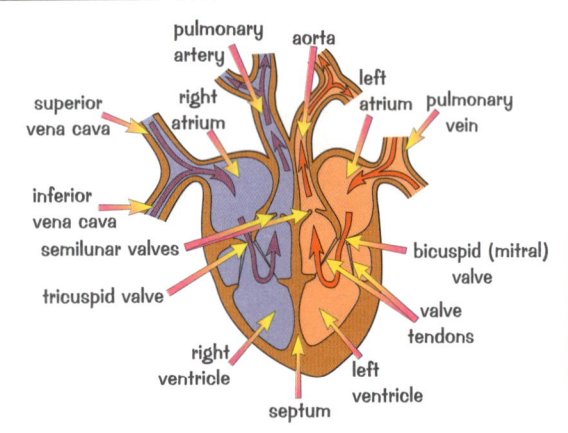

oxygenated blood has more oxygen — it's found in all arteries (except the pulmonary artery).

deoxygenated blood has less oxygen — it's found in all veins (except the pulmonary vein).

The stroke volume is the amount of blood pumped per beat. You can use it to work out the amount pumped per minute:

CARDIAC OUTPUT = STROKE VOLUME × HEART RATE

Each time a blood cell goes right round your body, it goes through the heart twice — that's double circulation. It happens because there are two circuits:

The systemic circuit is the main circuit. It carries:
1) oxygenated blood around the body in the arteries.
2) deoxygenated blood back to the heart along the veins
— this then gets reoxygenated in the pulmonary circuit.

The pulmonary circuit includes the heart and lungs. It carries:
1) deoxygenated blood from the heart to the lungs to be oxygenated. The blood then goes back to the heart to be pumped around the systemic circuit.

The Blood is Under Pressure

Your pulse is just the increase and decrease in pressure in the artery as your heart pumps blood. Blood pressure can be measured using a sphygmomanometer. It gives two readings:

SYSTOLIC PRESSURE — the pressure of the blood in the arteries when the left ventricle contracts.
DIASTOLIC PRESSURE — the pressure of the blood in the arteries when the left ventricle relaxes.

The heart — it's all just pump and circumstance...

That cardiac output equation's pretty easy to remember — as long as you understand it. Make sure you can draw that circulation diagram and label it properly — you really do need to know the order blood flows though the heart, and where the oxygenated and deoxygenated blood goes.

Section One — The Human Body

The Circulation

Blood is made up of blood cells and plasma and moves around the body in blood vessels.

Blood Pressure is Affected by Loads of Things

AGE — blood pressure tends to increase with age.
GENDER — generally higher in men.
EXERCISE — increases blood pressure in the short term, but reduces it in the long term.
STRESS — increases blood pressure.
If your blood pressure remains high, you're at higher risk of these:
ANGINA — sharp pains in the chest, caused by the heart not getting enough oxygen,
HEART ATTACKS — the heart stopping because of oxygen starvation,
STROKES — damage to the brain because of oxygen starvation.

There are Three Types of Blood Vessel...

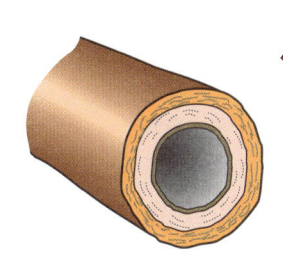

ARTERIES
Carry oxygenated blood away from the heart (except the pulmonary artery). Have thick, strong and elastic walls to cope with the pressure. Small arteries are called arterioles.

VEINS
Carry deoxygenated blood back to the heart (except the pulmonary vein). Have thinner walls than arteries because the blood is at a lower pressure. Veins have valves to keep the blood going in the right direction. Small veins are called venules.

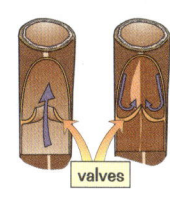

CAPILLARIES
Carry food and oxygen directly to the tissues, and take waste away from them. Very small with very thin walls.

...and Cells, Platelets and Plasma

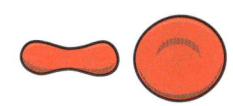

RED BLOOD CELLS
Carry oxygen around the body in red haemoglobin.
They have no nucleus, leaving more space for haemoglobin.

WHITE BLOOD CELLS
Fight against disease by destroying:
1) bacteria using antibodies,
2) toxins using antitoxins,
3) foreign microbes by consuming them.

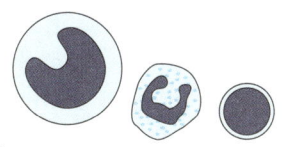

PLASMA CARRIES EVERYTHING
in the bloodstream. That includes:
1) Blood cells,
2) Digested food (e.g. glucose),
3) Waste (e.g. urea, carbon dioxide),
4) Hormones.

PLATELETS
Small fragments of cells with no nucleus.
Platelets help the blood to clot at wounds.

Vessel test you — loads of gory details to learn...

Okay, it's not too bad a page really. All nicely broken down into little bits. As usual, just take it a section at a time and make darn sure you can scribble it all down without looking. Enjoy...

Section One — The Human Body

Revision Summary for Section One

Right, it's the end of the first section — well, almost. You could just call it day and go on to the next section, but I wouldn't recommend it. Now's the perfect time to test what you've learnt, and reinforce it in your brain. It really won't take that long either — and it's certainly a lot quicker than not doing it and then having to relearn it all later. Right, here's a load of questions then. Don't expect to be able to answer them all straight away, but do aim to be able to answer them all eventually. Just look through them every now and then, and in no time you'll be able to go through the lot with no hesitation (and no cheating)...

1) Draw a rough sketch of the human skeleton and label as many bones as you can. You should be able to stick 23 labels on it.
2) Name five functions of bones.
3) Bones are divided into four types depending on their shape. Name the four different types.
4) Draw a spine and label the different kinds of vertebra. How many are there of each?
5) What type of connective tissue joins bones to bones? And what's the point of cartilage?
6) Draw a picture of: a) a fixed joint, b) a slightly movable joint, and c) a freely movable joint. Don't forget to label all the various bits.
7) Name five types of movement at a joint (Make sure you can give their proper names as well as describe them).
8) Name five types of movable joint. Give an example of each type.
9) Say what kinds of movement each type of movable joint will allow.
10) What do muscles and joints act as: a) levers, b) pulleys, or c) cranes?
11) Name the three different types of muscle, and give an example of each type. What are the differences between them?
12) What are the main muscles of the human body? Either label a sketch, or make sure you can name them on your own body. You should be able to name 11 muscles.
13) What are the differences between fast twitch and slow twitch muscle fibres? (And I don't mean just the obvious difference.) Name some sports that each type is suited to.
14) Are muscles attached to bones by: a) ligaments, b) tendons, c) cartilage, or d) sheep?
15) What's the fancy name for where a muscle attaches to a point on: a) a stationary bone, and b) a moving bone?
16) An antagonist relaxes while an agonist does work. TRUE or FALSE?
17) What's a synergist, and what does it do?
18) What are isotonic and isometric contractions?
19) What is muscle atrophy? And what is cramp?
20) Draw a rough sketch of the chest cavity, and mark on all the bits of the respiratory system.
21) Where does gaseous exchange take place? What gases are exchanged?
22) How are the air you breathe in and the air you breathe out different?
23) What are the technical terms for breathing in and breathing out?
24) Draw a diagram to show how you breathe in, and another one to show how you breathe out.
25) Explain these terms: a) tidal volume, b) vital capacity, c) residual volume.
26) What does your VO_2 measure? What does VO_2 Max mean?
27) Name three functions of the circulatory system.
28) Draw a diagram showing the heart and the two circuits that the blood travels round.
29) What are the two readings given when blood pressure is measured? Why are they different?
30) Name four things that affect blood pressure, and three things you're at risk of if your blood pressure is high.
31) Name the three main types of blood vessel.
32) Name the three types of blood cells. What does each of them do? What's the liquid called that makes up the rest of the blood?

Section One — The Human Body

Section Two — Health and Fitness

Health

Health is what everyone wants. You should be able to say what health actually is, and some of the things that can affect it — either for better or worse. Here we go...

Health is a State of Well-being

Remember this definition of health — it's the one used by the World Health Organisation (WHO).

"Health is a state of complete physical, mental and social well-being, and not merely the absence of disease or infirmity."

PHYSICAL WELL-BEING:
1) Your heart, kidneys, and the rest of your body are working well.
2) You're not suffering from any diseases.
3) You don't have any injuries.

MENTAL WELL-BEING:
1) You don't have too much stress or anxiety.
2) You're not suffering from any mental illnesses.
3) You feel content.

SOCIAL WELL-BEING:
1) You have food, clothing and shelter.
2) You have friends.
3) You believe you have some worth in society.

For Health, Remember PLEASED

There are quite a few things that can affect your health. You need to know what they are, and the effects each one has. If you learn PLEASED, you won't go far wrong. Simple really.

P → PERSONAL HYGIENE: Keep yourself clean — it'll help you to avoid loads of diseases. It won't do your social life any harm, either.

L → LIFESTYLE: This is everything you do — including your job and your hobbies. A healthy lifestyle will include some physical exercise, and some time to relax.

Rick always felt happiest when he could gaze at his tractor.

E → EMOTIONAL HEALTH: Feeling good is important. Try to avoid too much stress and worry. This can be caused by friends and relationships as well as things like work.

A → ALCOHOL / DRUG USE: Misuse of substances can lead to poor health. That includes alcohol and tobacco. Even breathing in other people's smoke (passive smoking) can lead to poor health.

S → SAFETY: If you have a dangerous job or hobby, you're more likely to injure yourself. So use the proper safety equipment — and in sport, play by the rules.

E → ENVIRONMENT: Pollution can cause respiratory problems. Noise can cause stress and affect your sleep.

D → DIET: You need the right balance of nutrients so you can cope with your lifestyle.

If you've got a dangerous hobby — make sure you know what you're doing.

I'm very PLEASED to have finished this page...

There's a lot more to health than just not being ill — and that's something you'll need to be aware of in the exam. The stuff that can affect health is easy to learn if you just remember the PLEASED rule — but test yourself regularly to check you still know what the letters stand for.

Fitness

There are two different kinds of fitness — and you need to know about both of them. It'll also be important to know what factors can affect fitness.

Fitness can be General or Specific

There are two basic kinds of fitness — general fitness, and specific fitness.

GENERAL FITNESS:

This means you're healthy, and can do everyday activities without feeling too tired. For this, you need the four S's.

1) Strength	3) Stamina
2) Speed	4) Suppleness

General fitness also includes:
1) Cardiovascular endurance (aerobic fitness) — so your muscles can get enough oxygen to work properly.
2) Muscular endurance — so your muscles don't get tired too quickly.
3) Good body composition — you shouldn't be too fat or too thin.

SPECIFIC FITNESS:

This is fitness to play a sport at a high level — and it needs good general fitness, as well as some or all of these...

1) Agility — to change direction quickly.
2) Balance — so you don't fall over.
3) Coordination — to move accurately and smoothly.
4) Explosive strength — brute strength combined with speed.
5) Fast reactions — to respond quickly.
6) Good timing — so you can act at just the right moment.

You'll need coordination and balance for one-legged plate spinning.

These are almost the first seven letters of the alphabet — ABC-EFG. Only 'D' is missing.

Fitness is Affected by HIP DAD

You can control some factors affecting fitness, but not others. Learn these HIP DAD factors.

H → HEIGHT, WEIGHT & SOMATOTYPE — Your basic shape can affect how good you can become at certain activities.

I → ILLNESS & INJURY — They can affect fitness, either temporarily or permanently.

P → PSYCHOLOGICAL FACTORS — The stress and tension of preparing for a big competition are examples of these.

Hey, it's got a great beat.

D → DISABILITIES — They can affect fitness. But by concentrating on particular activities, you can still reach a high level of fitness.

A → ALCOHOL, DRUGS & SMOKING — They all have a negative effect on health and general fitness, in both the short- and long-term.

D → DIET — This needs to contain the right balance of the different types of nutrient.

Cardiovascular Fitness and Muscular Fitness

Cardiovascular (CV) fitness and muscular fitness are things you need to know about for the exam.

CARDIOVASCULAR FITNESS

This is about keeping your muscles supplied with oxygen.

If your heart and lungs can provide a lot of oxygen, your CV fitness (or CV endurance) is good.

MUSCULAR FITNESS

This is good if your muscles can apply a lot of force to something.

Basically, this means you can push, pull, lift, throw etc. very hard or very quickly.

Remember — there are 4 S's in fitnessss...

This page is full of memory aids: 'the 4 S's', 'ABC-EFG' and 'HIP DAD'. It's memory-aid-tastic, in fact. But they do really help — so use them. It'll help if you keep a separate note of all these aids, along with a note of what they're helping you to remember — so you don't get confused.

Section Two — Health and Fitness

Exercise

Exercise is good for you — but you need to know why it's good for you, and what guidelines you should follow while doing it. Learn what affects the amount of exercise different people need as well.

Exercise Helps Physically, Mentally and Socially

There are loads of very good reasons for exercising. These reasons fall into three basic groups:

PHYSICAL BENEFITS:
1) Improves your body shape, muscle tone and posture.
2) Strengthens the bones, reduces the chances of illness and increases life expectancy.
3) Increases your strength, endurance, flexibility and overall fitness.

MENTAL BENEFITS:
1) Gives you a challenge to aim for.
2) Helps you deal with stress and tension, and it can be fun.
3) Helps you to feel better about yourself and increase your self-confidence.

SOCIAL BENEFITS:
1) Can improve your teamwork and cooperation.
2) Can help you meet people and lead to new friendships.
3) Sport can also improve your image and bring in money.

Stressed? Me? Don't be ridiculous.

Different People Need Different Amounts of Exercise

Not everyone will need (or want) the same amount of exercise. It all depends on a person's...

PHYSICAL CONDITION:
It's good to take things easy or see a doctor before starting to exercise if you've...
1) Not exercised for quite a long time,
2) Been ill for a while,
3) Reached middle age.

LONG-TERM GOALS:
You'll need different amounts of exercise, depending on what your goal is...
1) To walk up stairs without feeling out of breath,
2) To do a 5-mile fun run,
3) To win an Olympic gold medal for rowing.

Exercise Doesn't Have to be Hell

You can hurt yourself exercising if you're not careful. Here are some guidelines that should help...

1) Exercise should be regular — so establish a routine. Exercising 4 times a week for 20 minutes will really help.
2) Start with gentle exercises and increase the intensity as you get fitter.
3) Don't overdo it. You shouldn't feel there's 'no gain without pain'. That's not true.

Charity Fun Run — I just don't understand it. I played tennis back in 1958.

Don't play tennis once and expect to be fit for life.

You can get good exercise by just changing a few bad habits...
1) Walk or cycle short distances, instead of taking a bus or going by car.
2) Don't take the lift — use the stairs.

Or you could get fitter by using a rope suspended from an upstairs window instead of taking the lift.

Don't take the lift — other people need it...

All three sections here are important. Learn one section at a time by covering the page and writing down what you can remember. And check you can still remember the stuff the next day — and then the next week, and so on. Don't learn it once and assume you'll still know it in the exam.

Section Two — Health and Fitness

The Effects of Exercise

When you start to exercise, your body has to make sure that your muscles get the oxygen they need so they can keep working. It also has to avoid overheating. It's all clever stuff.

Your Body Moves Up a Gear When You Exercise

To keep your muscles supplied with oxygen, these changes 'kick in' when you start to exercise.

① When you exercise, your muscles start to produce more carbon dioxide and need more oxygen...

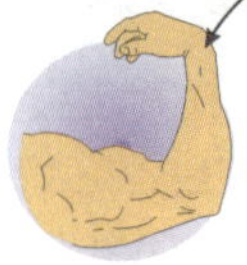

② ...so you start to breathe more deeply and quickly.

③ ...and your heart beats faster to circulate more oxygenated blood.

④ Your arterioles widen to stop your blood pressure getting too high...

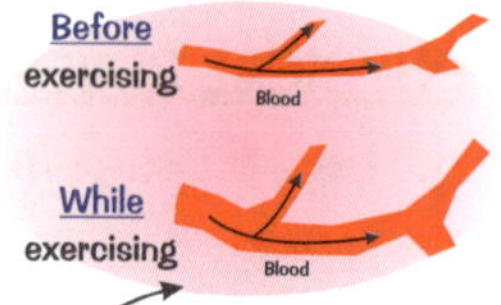

Adrenaline (a hormone) is released when you exercise. It's the adrenaline that causes all these changes (② to ⑥).

⑤ ...and to make the most of your blood supply, blood that would usually go to organs like the gut and liver is diverted to the muscles...

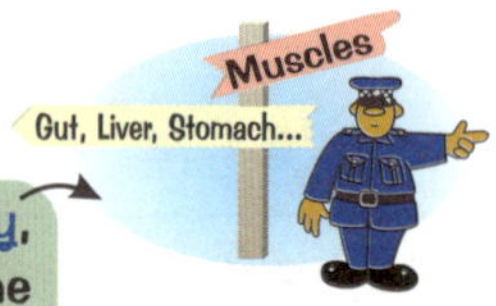

⑥ ...by blood vessels either widening (vasodilation) or constricting (vasoconstriction).

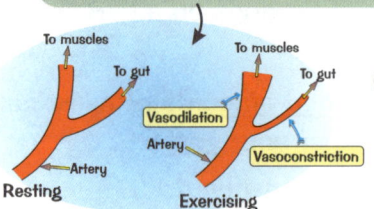

⑦ Contracting muscles squeeze your veins — 'squirting' blood back to your heart more quickly...

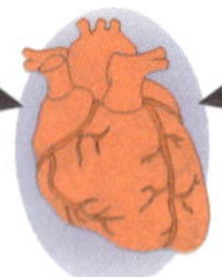

⑧ ...and, as the heart's a bit elastic, it stretches, and then contracts more strongly to pump even more blood.

Which is why your heart seems to thump.

A Also, as your muscles work, they generate heat — which warms your blood...

B ...and so this blood is shunted closer to your skin, so the heat can escape through radiation.

C And you also start to sweat, which helps keep you cool.

Which makes you go red.

'Shunting' blood means diverting it to where it's most needed.

Recovery Time Depends on Fitness

After all that, it takes a while to return to normal when you stop:

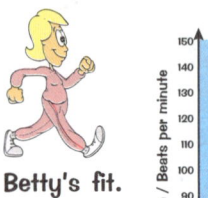

Betty's fit. 
Ed's unfit.

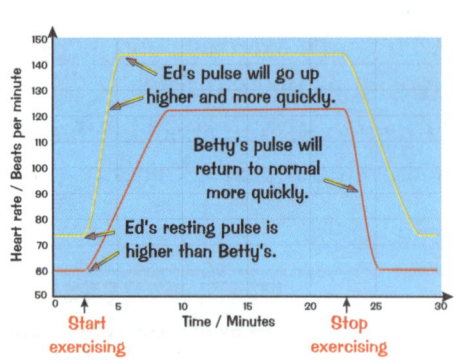

Ed's pulse will go up higher and more quickly.
Betty's pulse will return to normal more quickly.
Ed's resting pulse is higher than Betty's.

HEART RATE
When you stop exercising, your heart rate falls to its normal rate. The fitter you are, the faster it falls.

RECOVERY TIME
This depends on
1) How strenuous the exercise was,
2) How fit you are.

GLYCOGEN STORES
It takes up to 48 hours to replace the glycogen used up.

MUSCLE REPAIR
Muscles may get slightly damaged during exercise, and need to be repaired.

LACTIC ACID REMOVAL
You still need lots of oxygen when you stop exercising to get rid of lactic acid — you must 'repay' the oxygen debt.

Get yourself in gear — or it could be embarrassing...

The first section's really important. It's easier to remember it if you imagine yourself exercising — heart thumping, gasping for breath, red in the face etc. Then imagine what actually makes your face go red, and so on. It's also dead important that you learn about the 'shunt' of blood towards muscles when you exercise. Know why and how it happens. It's amazing, I reckon.

Section Two — Health and Fitness

The Effects of Exercise

Exercise makes your body change in more permanent ways too. The positive effects of regular exercise stay with you long after the end of the exercise session. All the stuff you need is here.

Aerobic Training Helps Your Breathing and Circulation

Aerobic training, where your heart and lungs work hard for a long time, does your circulatory and respiratory systems a power of good.

CIRCULATORY SYSTEM:
1) Your body makes more red blood cells — so it can transport more oxygen.
2) Your arteries get bigger and 'stretchier' — so your blood pressure falls.
3) More capillaries form in your muscles, so oxygen is delivered more efficiently.
4) Your heart gets bigger (just like when you exercise other muscles), and the walls of the heart get a bit thicker.
5) After exercising, your heart rate falls more quickly to its resting level.

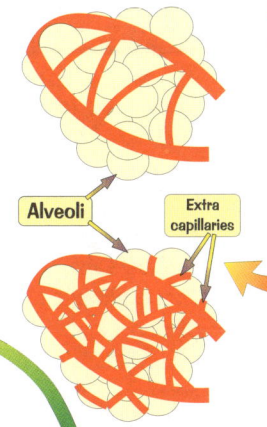

After exercising, Bob also falls quickly to his resting level.

RESPIRATORY SYSTEM:
1) The diaphragm and intercostal muscles get stronger — so they can make your chest cavity larger.
2) With a larger chest cavity, you can breathe more air in — so your vital capacity increases.
3) More capillaries grow around the alveoli — so more carbon dioxide and oxygen can be swapped at any time.
4) Because gas exchange is quicker, you can keep up vigorous exercise for longer.

A bigger heart means a bigger stroke volume, and so your heart can beat more slowly and still pump the same amount of blood.

Training is also Good For You in Loads of Other Ways

It's not just aerobic training that does you good — other kinds of exercise are also beneficial.

ENDURANCE TRAINING:
1) Makes your body better at using fat for energy.
2) Makes your muscles more efficient at using oxygen.
3) Increases your VO₂ Max — the amount of oxygen your body can use in a minute.
4) Makes more capillaries form around your muscles, so they can get more oxygen.

The process of making more capillaries is called capillarisation.

STRENGTH TRAINING:
1) Makes your muscles thicker so they can contract more strongly — this thickening is called hypertrophy.
2) Makes your tendons bigger and stronger.

ANAEROBIC TRAINING:
1) Makes the walls of the heart thicker (they're only muscle, after all).
2) Makes your muscles able to put up with lactic acid for longer — and they also get better at getting rid of it.

Boring trophy

Number 1 Hypertrophy

And exercise helps your body in yet more ways. Read and learn this stuff, too.

JOINTS:
1) Exercise makes your ligaments stronger, and your cartilage thicker.
2) Regular stretching improves your flexibility.

BONES:
Exercise makes your bones stronger.

It's true.

BODY FAT:
When you train regularly, fat is burnt more quickly — whether you're exercising or resting — so you get slimmer.

Train that brain — start by learning this page...

If you remember ABC, you'll be able to remember this first section — Aerobic training helps Breathing and Circulation. As for the other stuff — cover the page and see if you can write down the various headings first. Then learn one section at a time, otherwise you'll get it all confused.

Section Two — Health and Fitness

Diet and Nutrition

"You are what you eat," people sometimes say — that's how <u>vital</u> this subject is. It's very important to know about different foods, <u>what</u> they contain, and <u>why</u> we need to eat them.

You need a Balance of Protein, Carbohydrate and Fat

Protein, carbohydrate and fat make up the bulk of your food. They provide the <u>energy</u>.

PROTEINS — ABOUT 15% OF CALORIES:

1) Help the body <u>grow</u> and <u>repair itself</u>.
2) Found in foods like <u>meat</u>, <u>fish</u>, <u>eggs</u>, <u>milk</u> and <u>soya beans</u>.
3) Made from chemicals called <u>amino acids</u> — there are two different types:
   a) <u>Non-essential Amino Acids</u> — your body can make these.
   b) <u>Essential Amino Acids</u> — your body can't make these, so you have to eat enough of them.

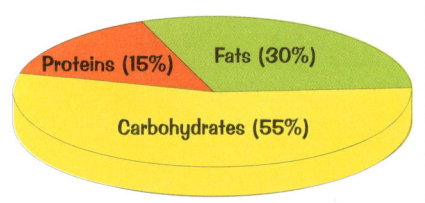

Pie chart: Proteins (15%), Fats (30%), Carbohydrates (55%)

About how much of each nutrient we should eat (by <u>calorie intake</u>, not weight)

CARBOHYDRATES — ABOUT 55% OF CALORIES:

Provide <u>energy</u>.
   a) <u>Simple Carbohydrates</u> (e.g. sugar) In sweets, jam and cakes. You shouldn't eat too much of these.
   b) <u>Complex Carbohydrates</u> (e.g. starch) In bread, pasta, rice and potatoes and cereals. These should be the biggest part of any meal.

1) <u>Carbohydrase enzymes</u> in the gut break down complex carbohydrates into simple ones (i.e. glucose), which then enter the <u>bloodstream</u>.
2) Some of the glucose is used directly for energy around the body.
3) The rest is converted to <u>glycogen</u> and stored in the <u>liver</u> and <u>muscles</u>.

FATS — ABOUT 30% OF CALORIES:

Provide <u>energy</u> and keep us <u>warm</u>.
Contain chemicals called <u>fatty acids</u>.
   a) <u>Saturated Fatty Acids</u> (Saturates) Found mainly in animal products.
   b) <u>Monosaturated Fatty Acids</u> (Monounsaturates) Found in many foods, like olive oil.
   c) <u>Polyunsaturated Fatty Acids</u> (Polyunsaturates) Found in some margarines and oils, and oily fish.

You need Small Amounts of Vitamins and Minerals too

VITAMINS

1) Help your bones, teeth, and skin to <u>grow</u>.
2) Needed for many of the body's <u>chemical reactions</u>.

A) FAT-SOLUBLE VITAMINS:

Can be stored in the body:
   a) <u>Vitamin A</u> — handy for <u>growth</u> and <u>night vision</u>, and found in vegetables, eggs and liver.
   b) <u>Vitamin D</u> — handy for strong bones, so you don't get <u>rickets</u>. Made by the skin in sunshine, but also found in milk, fish, liver and eggs.

B) WATER-SOLUBLE VITAMINS:

Can't be stored, so you need to eat them <u>regularly</u>:
   a) <u>Vitamin C</u> — good for your skin, gums and connective tissue; you get <u>scurvy</u> without it. Found in fruit and veg. — especially citrus fruit like oranges and lemons.

With a properly <u>balanced diet</u>, you don't need <u>vitamin supplements</u>.

MINERALS

1) Needed for healthy <u>bones</u> and <u>teeth</u>, and to build other <u>tissues</u>.
2) <u>Trace elements</u> are minerals you only need a little bit of.
3) Minerals help in various <u>chemical reactions</u> in the body.
   a) <u>Calcium</u> — needed for strong <u>bones</u> and <u>teeth</u>, but also for <u>muscle contraction</u>. Lots in green vegetables, milk, cheese and some fish.
   b) <u>Iron</u> — handy for <u>haemoglobin</u> in red blood cells; you get <u>anaemia</u> without it. There's tons in liver, beans and green vegetables.
   c) <u>Iodine</u> — needed for <u>thyroid hormones</u>; you get <u>goitre</u> without it (swollen thyroid gland in neck). Found in sea food, and vegetables grown in iodine-rich soils.

The National Lunchery — eat could be you...

There's a lot of stuff here, but at least it's all broken down into <u>nice small pieces</u>. Try learning the <u>main points</u> first — like the five kinds of nutrients. Then for each nutrient, make sure you can scribble down those points. Learn it <u>a bit at a time</u> and it won't seem so bad...

Section Two — Health and Fitness

Diet and Nutrition

You need to get the right balance of food, just like with anything else in life. The trouble is, getting the balance right can be a bit tricky...

Water and Dietary Fibre are just as Important

Only protein, carbohydrate, fat, vitamins and minerals are really nutrients. But they're definitely not the only things you need. You'd have pretty major problems without these two...

WATER
1) Water's needed in loads of chemical reactions in the body. It's also lost in your breath, sweat, urine and faeces.
2) If you don't drink enough to replace what your body uses or loses you'll become dehydrated, and you won't perform as well.
3) If you drink too much, your kidneys will produce more urine to get rid of the excess.

Not the best way to increase your fibre intake

DIETARY FIBRE
1) Fibre's not a nutrient either, but you need it to keep your digestive system working properly.
2) There's lots of fibre in fruit and vegetables — another good reason to eat loads of them.

A Balanced Diet — all the Nutrients in the Right Amounts

1) A balanced diet is one that contains all the nutrients you need in the right amounts for good health.
2) A good way to achieve this is to eat a varied diet with plenty of fruit and vegetables, but not too much fat.
3) People often talk about food groups. Including food from each group below can help to get a balanced diet.

(though the last two groups aren't essential)

Bread, Nuts, Cereals, Pulses, Potatoes  | Fruit and Vegetables  | Meat and Fish  | Dairy Foods

Eat Different Diets for Different Sports

Different sports place different demands on the body. That's why top athletes eat specific foods.

1) **WEIGHTLIFTERS / SPRINTERS**
Need muscle power, so they'll need lots of protein for muscle growth.

2) **GYMNASTS**
Need to be strong, but small and light. They need a good balance of carbohydrates, proteins and fats.

3) **MARATHON RUNNERS**
Need endurance over long periods, so they should get plenty of carbohydrates.

Organise Your Meals Around Activities

It's important to eat at the right times if you want to perform well at sport.

BEFORE AN ACTIVITY
Top athletes increase carbohydrate intake a few days before an event. This increases the amount of glycogen stored in the muscles, giving them plenty of energy. It's called carbohydrate loading.

DURING AN ACTIVITY
You shouldn't eat while exercising — your digestive system may not be able to cope. But you should drink to replace lost fluid.

AFTER AN ACTIVITY
Continue replacing lost fluid, but don't eat immediately. After a couple of hours, you should start eating to replace used energy.

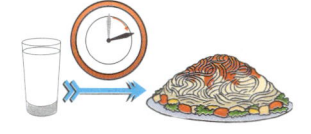

Food for sport — runner beans...

Again lots of stuff here, but it's all in little chunks. Each one's a doddle by itself, so just take it easy and do a bit at a time. Soon you'll be reeling those facts off like no one's business...

Section Two — Health and Fitness

Energy

All this energy lark's pretty straightforward really. Eat as many calories as you use up and you'll stay the same weight. Well, okay, maybe there's a little more to it than that...

Fats, Carbohydrates and Proteins Give You Energy

Fats, carbohydrates and proteins give us energy — the amount of energy is the energy value.

The energy needed to keep the heart beating and the body breathing is the Basal Metabolic Rate — or BMR.

Energy value is measured in kilojoules (kJ) or kilocalories (kcal) — but people usually say calories instead of kilocalories.

Total Energy needed = BMR + Energy used to work, play etc.

If you eat more than you need, the extra energy is stored as adipose tissue (i.e. fat) — and you gain weight.

If you eat less than you need, your body uses its reserves of adipose tissue, and you lose weight.

Eating too much can lead to obesity, which is when someone has at least 20% more body fat than the norm for their height and build. Obesity places a lot of strain on the heart and muscles.

Anorexia is a mental illness. Sufferers refuse to eat and become dangerously thin. They often have a distorted image of their own body — still thinking they need to lose weight.

Different People Need Different Amounts of Food

You need to know how different factors affect how much food different people will need.

1) AGE — If you're growing, you need to eat more. Adults generally need less food.

2) LIFESTYLE — An office worker needs less food than a builder.

3) SPORTS PLAYED — Eat more if you play strenuous sports.

4) SIZE & SEX — The bigger you are, the more food you need — and men usually need more food than women for a given size.

Weight Control — Exercise and a Balanced Diet

Many people try to lose weight by just cutting down on the calories — but that rarely works. Just eating less of the same thing but doing nothing else different isn't the best way to lose weight.

There are two keys to losing weight, and it works much better with both together:

1) Eat a more balanced diet — it's especially important not to overdo the fat. This might involve making a permanent change to the types of food you eat.

2) Get plenty of exercise. This bit's really important — partly because you'll use up calories exercising, but mainly because it'll increase your basal metabolic rate (BMR), so you'll use up more calories when resting too. Exercise also suppresses the appetite, so you won't want to eat as much.

Body composition is a measure of body fat — it's the percentage of your weight that's fat.

Fat's your lot — so what are you weighting for...

Your Basal Metabolic Rate shows how much energy you need — it's like a car's miles per gallon. Make sure that you know what things can affect it — like age, lifestyle, size, and sex. And you've got to know how to lose weight sensibly with a balanced diet — so that'll include some exercise...

Section Two — Health and Fitness

Endurance

How long your muscles can work for depends on your endurance — you need to know about the two kinds of endurance. You also need to learn about the ways the body converts food into energy.

Muscular Endurance is Linked to Strength

You've got muscular endurance if your muscles can keep exerting a lot of force for a long time.

1) When your muscles can't work properly any more, your arms and legs start to feel heavy or weak, and muscle fatigue sets in.

2) Slow twitch muscle fibres get tired less quickly — so it's easier to improve your muscular endurance if you've got loads of slow twitch fibres.

To improve muscular endurance, you need to get stronger — weight training is a good way to do this.

Cardiovascular Endurance is Linked to Heart and Lungs

Cardiovascular (CV) endurance is how good you are at keeping your muscles supplied with oxygen. This is the job of your heart and lungs.

1) As your muscles work harder, they need more oxygen — so your breathing and heart rate get faster to move more oxygen around the body.

2) The more efficient your cardiovascular system, the slower your pulse rate will be (either resting or exercising), and the quicker it will return to normal after you've been exercising.

3) To improve your CV endurance, you have to work your heart and lungs hard for at least 15 minutes. Make sure your pulse is in the aerobic or target zones. Then your VO_2 will be between 55% and 75% of your VO_2 Max (see p7).

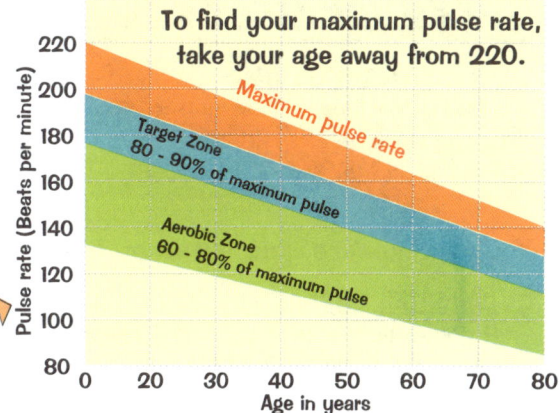

To find your maximum pulse rate, take your age away from 220.

Maximum pulse rate
Target Zone 80 - 90% of maximum pulse
Aerobic Zone 60 - 80% of maximum pulse

Pulse rate (Beats per minute) vs Age in years

Glucose can be Converted into Energy in Two Ways

Respiration is the process that takes place in living cells to release energy from food molecules. There are two kinds of respiration — aerobic and anaerobic. They both convert glucose into energy. Which one the body uses depends on the intensity of the activity:

AEROBIC RESPIRATION — with oxygen

1) During aerobic activity, your heart and lungs supply your muscles with plenty of oxygen.

Glucose + Oxygen ➡ Carbon dioxide + Water + Energy

2) You breathe out the carbon dioxide through your lungs, while the water is lost as sweat, urine, or in the air you breathe out.

3) As long as your muscles are supplied with enough oxygen, you can do aerobic exercise — so this is used for long periods of exercise.

This is how marathon runners get their energy.

ANAEROBIC RESPIRATION — without oxygen

1) During anaerobic activity, your muscles are not supplied with enough oxygen.

Glucose + No oxygen ➡ Lactic acid + Energy

2) This lactic acid builds up if there's a shortage of oxygen (this shortage of oxygen is called an oxygen debt).

3) Lactic acid is a mild poison and its build-up soon makes your muscles feel tired — so this is used for short, strenuous activities.

This is how sprinters get their energy.

Learn about endurance — if you can take it...

The aerobic system is much more efficient, so the body uses it whenever it can. The trouble is, it's not that fast. If the body can't get enough oxygen to the muscles, it has to use the anaerobic system.

Section Two — Health and Fitness

Strength, Speed and Power

Strength, speed and power are closely linked — but they're all a bit different. Here's what they actually are, and why they're needed...

Static, Explosive and Dynamic Strength

There are three kinds of strength. Learn them well — and what you need them for.

STATIC STRENGTH
1) You use static strength to exert force on an immovable object.
2) Muscles stay the same length, so there's not much movement.
3) Useful in arm-wrestling and a rugby scrum.

EXPLOSIVE STRENGTH
1) You use explosive strength to exert force in one very short, but very fast movement.
2) Closely linked to power.
3) Useful for the javelin or high jump.

DYNAMIC STRENGTH
1) You use dynamic strength to apply force repeatedly over a long time.
2) Linked to endurance.
3) Useful for doing loads of press-ups or cycling.

Most sports need all three kinds of strength — but they're usually not all equally important.

Speed Means Reacting and Moving

REACTION TIME
This is the time it takes you to respond to something. It could be a starter's gun, or a pass in football.

For speed, you need:
1) Fast reaction times,
2) Fast movement times.

MOVEMENT TIME
And this is the time it takes you to carry out a certain movement — e.g. a 100 m sprint, or a shot at goal.

You can increase your speed by training, but certain factors limit how successful you can be...

1) **INHERITED CHARACTERISTICS**
   If you're born with a lot of fast twitch muscle fibres, it's easier to increase your speed.

   Increase speed by increasing your strength, or by improving your action — e.g. improve your tennis serve or golf swing.

2) **BODY SHAPE & SIZE**
   Your bone structure, weight, and muscle size put limits on how much you can increase your speed.

   This time, I'm gonna beat that hare fair and square.

   If your reactions are slow, it doesn't matter how fast you can move.

3) **DURATION OF EVENT**
   It's just not possible to run flat-out forever — everybody slows down pretty soon. For longer distances, it's better to improve your endurance.

Power Means Speed and Strength Together

Power is speed and strength combined — and there's a strong link between power and explosive strength. Most sports need power for some things — even ones like golf, where it's not obvious.

I have the power.

SPORT	YOU NEED POWER TO...
Football	...shoot
Golf	...drive
Table tennis	...smash
Tennis	...serve and smash
Cricket	...bowl fast and bat

Coordination and balance also help generate power — it's not just strength you need.

Strong, powerful, handsome — but enough about me...

Another page with lots on it. The names of the different kinds of strength give you clues about the differences between them. Power's just a combination of what's in the first two bits of this page, so there's not really anything new in the last bit. Make sure all this stuff is in your head.

Section Two — Health and Fitness

Flexibility

Flexibility, suppleness, mobility — they're all the same thing. They're all to do with how far your joints move — and this depends on the type of joint and the 'stretchiness' of the muscles around it.

Flexibility has Many Benefits

It's often forgotten about, but suppleness is dead useful for any sport. Here's why...

1) **STRETCHES GET YOU READY TO WORK:**
Stretching is a good way to warm up and get your body ready to work.

2) **BETTER PERFORMANCE:**
You can't do some sports without being flexible — gymnastics, for example.
Flexibility makes you more efficient in other sports like swimming or hurdling — so you use less energy.

3) **FEWER INJURIES:**
If you're flexible, you're less likely to pull or strain a muscle or stretch too far and injure yourself.

4) **BETTER POSTURE:**
More flexibility means a better posture and fewer aches and pains.
Bad posture can lead to permanent deformity of the spine, as well as straining the abdominal muscles and back.
It can also impair breathing — another way that flexibility affects performance.

Stretching after exercising helps prevent muscle soreness.

He'll bend over backwards to help you, you know.
So I've heard.

Work Towards All-Round Flexibility

Flexibility in these joints is especially important because they're used all the time in sport:

BACK:
Most movements need flexibility here.
It's often injured because not many people have supple backs.

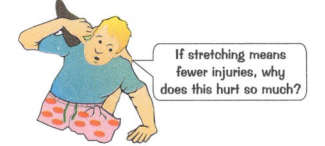

It took me years to get this supple.

If stretching means fewer injuries, why does this hurt so much?

HIP:
Anything involving raising or lowering a leg needs you to bend at the hip.
Not many people are flexible here. It's a good place to test flexibility.

LEGS:
Flexibility at the knee and ankle is important for running or kicking.
Most people are pretty supple here through walking.

Strength training can limit flexibility — so do plenty of stretching exercises as well.

For more about fitness testing, see pages 34 & 35.

SHOULDERS & ARMS:
Flexibility here helps with a lot of sports — like throwing and swimming.
Most people stretch these joints getting dressed in the morning.

Active or Passive Stretches Improve Flexibility

Flexibility's a good thing, so you should know how to improve it. In a nutshell, you need to move the joint past where it would normally go, but there are two ways to do that:

ACTIVE STRETCHING:
1) You do the work of stretching your muscles — slowly and gently.
2) If it hurts, or if your muscles start to shake, ease up.
3) Don't bounce into a stretch because you can tear muscle fibres.

I think I need to wash my feet.

PASSIVE STRETCHING:
1) A partner does the work of stretching your muscles.
2) Tell him or her straight away if you feel any pain.

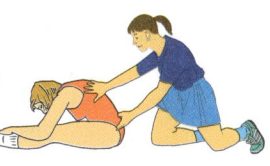

Flexibility — it's enough to drive you loopy...

Knowing the benefits of flexibility will be important in the exam — but also make sure you know the dangers of stretching incorrectly. And don't be confused by the three different names for flexibility — suppleness and mobility are exactly the same thing. Get learning, and have fun.

Section Two — Health and Fitness

Age and Gender

A person's *age* and *gender* will affect how well they can play most sports. Usually (but *not* always) men and women have *separate* competitions — while children don't often compete against adults.

Age Affects Performance in Sport

Age affects performance in loads of different ways. Make sure you know how.

STRENGTH:
1) You don't reach your *maximum* strength until you're *fully grown* — usually at about 20.
2) In your *20s and 30s*, it's still *easy* to *build* more *muscle*.
3) After this, protein levels and muscle mass *fall*, strength *declines* and it's harder to build muscle.

OXYGEN CAPACITY:
This *falls* as you get older — less oxygen can be taken to the muscles.

INJURY & DISEASE:
1) Older people are *more likely* to injure themselves.
2) It takes *longer* for an older person to *recover* from an injury.
3) Older people generally suffer *more* from *diseases* — cancer and heart disease, for example.

REACTION TIMES:
Your reactions get *slower* as you get older.

FLEXIBILITY:
1) People are *most flexible* in their *teens*.
2) After the age of about *30*, people generally start to become *less flexible*.

EXPERIENCE:
1) Experience is often a *vital* factor in sport.
2) As you get older, you *gain* more experience.

This is why there are often *age divisions* in competitions. An 8-year-old can't compete fairly in *most sports* against a 14-year-old. Similarly, people of 50 can't usually compete against people of 25.

Age Doesn't Matter for Some Sports

Lots of sports are thought of as 'for old people' or 'for young people'. This isn't always *fair*.

If a sport depends on *strength* or *endurance* (e.g. weightlifting or marathon running), older people will have a *disadvantage* — but for less strenuous sports (e.g. bowls), this doesn't have to be true.

You can *control* some of the effects of ageing (stretching can slow down the loss of flexibility), but *not* others.

Gender can affect Performance

As well as separating *young and old*, competitions usually split *men and women*. Here's why:

MEN & WOMEN HAVE DIFFERENT BODIES:
1) Men have a *longer, heavier* bone structure.
2) Women have a *wider, flatter pelvis* (which is better for childbearing).
3) Women generally have more *body fat* than men.
4) The *menstrual cycle* can affect performance.

Women are *discriminated* against in some sports — they get *less prize money*, and their events have a *lower profile*. See page 46 for more info.

GIRLS MATURE EARLIER THAN BOYS:
1) Girls reach *physical maturity* at 16 or 17.
2) Boys don't mature until about 20.

MEN ARE GENERALLY STRONGER:
Men have *bigger muscles*, due to higher *testosterone* levels.

WOMEN ARE GENERALLY MORE FLEXIBLE:
This is partly because they've got *less muscle*.

Revision should be the main thing on your age-gender...

Another page with lots on it that you just have to *remember*. Test yourself. Cover the page up and see if you can *write down* the ways that *age* and *gender* affect performance. And don't just learn it once — test yourself *regularly* before the exam so you don't forget. It's the *only* way.

Section Two — Health and Fitness

Somatotype

Somatotype means the basic shape of your body. Your somatotype can have a big effect on your suitability for a particular sport. Being the right shape is no guarantee of success, but it helps.

Somatotypes are Body Shapes

There are three basic somatotypes — ectomorph, mesomorph and endomorph. Everyone's body shape can be described by three numbers from 1 to 7 — one for each of the 3 basic somatotypes. Think of these basic somatotypes as extremes — at the corners of a triangular graph.

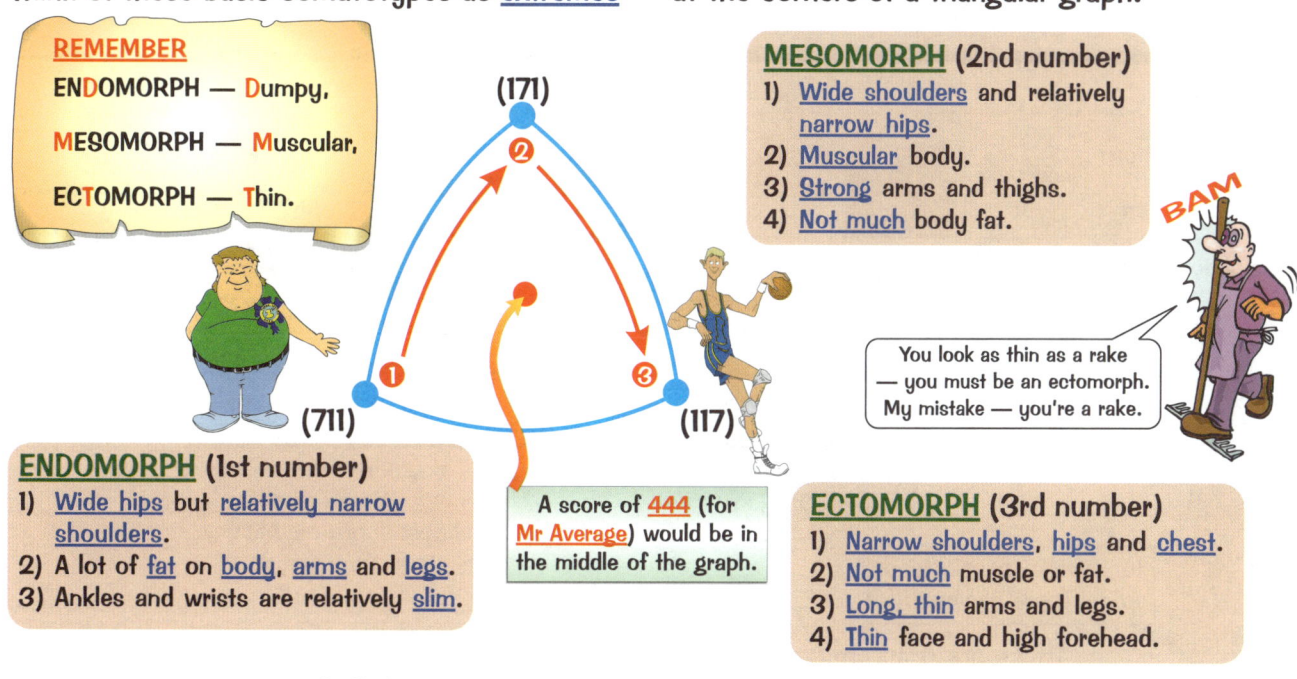

REMEMBER
EN**D**OMORPH — **D**umpy,
MESOMORPH — **M**uscular,
EC**T**OMORPH — **T**hin.

MESOMORPH (2nd number)
1) Wide shoulders and relatively narrow hips.
2) Muscular body.
3) Strong arms and thighs.
4) Not much body fat.

You look as thin as a rake — you must be an ectomorph. My mistake — you're a rake.

ENDOMORPH (1st number)
1) Wide hips but relatively narrow shoulders.
2) A lot of fat on body, arms and legs.
3) Ankles and wrists are relatively slim.

A score of 444 (for Mr Average) would be in the middle of the graph.

ECTOMORPH (3rd number)
1) Narrow shoulders, hips and chest.
2) Not much muscle or fat.
3) Long, thin arms and legs.
4) Thin face and high forehead.

Everyone is a mixture of all three basic body types — but people who play sport at a very high level tend to get high mesomorph scores, since strength is often important in sport.

Different Somatotypes Suit Different Sports

Sports are usually more suited to certain body types. So having a high number for the right body type, gives you a natural advantage:

Sumo wrestlers need strength, weight, and a low centre of gravity — strong endomorphic and mesomorphic features.

Who ate all the pies? Ah, it was me.

High jumpers need to be tall and light, but with powerful muscles — ectomorphic and mesomorphic features.

Ideal somatotypes for different sports.

ENDOMORPHS — suited to activities like wrestling and shot-putting.

MESOMORPHS — suited to activities like the decathlon, swimming, gymnastics and bodybuilding.

ECTOMORPHS — suited to activities like long distance running and high jumping.

"This will be the endomorph" — Tony Hart in exclusive interview...

Be sure to learn the word somatotype. It's a fancy word — but all it means is somebody's shape. And remember, nearly everybody is a mixture of the three basic body types. Learn the names well — it'd be a bad mistake to get the three basic somatotypes confused. Get your learning hat on.

Section Two — Health and Fitness

Sport and Personality

Your personality can influence the types of sport you prefer. If you're a quiet sort of person, you'll probably like different sports from someone who's louder. Get learning this stuff.

People with Different Personalities Prefer Different Sports

You can describe people's personalities by saying how extroverted or introverted they are. Some people can be called extroverts, and some called introverts. But this can be misleading, because no one is completely extroverted or introverted — they're just closer to one or the other.

This diagram shows the effect that personality has on people's choice of sport.

Introverted side: concentration, less pain, precision, calm, self-motivation, individual performance, thinking, less arousal, intricate skills

Extroverted side: activity, excitement, less thinking, less concentration, simple skills, team involvement, arousal, speed, more pain

Most people's personalities are somewhere in the middle.

If you're more introverted, you're going to choose more of these things in your sport.

If you're more extroverted, you're going to choose more of these things in your sport.

Introverted people tend to get more nervous...

These are only general rules — you'll be able to find loads of exceptions.

Aggression Has To Be Controlled

Aggression can have good and bad effects. It's good if it's kept under control — but bad if it means you break the rules or injure an opponent. There are two types of aggression.

INDIRECT AGGRESSION:
Indirect aggression means hitting objects (like a tennis ball or cricket ball).

DIRECT AGGRESSION:
Direct aggression is when there is actual physical contact between two competitors — like in boxing or rugby.

Aggression in some athletes — like swimmers — could be just a fierce determination to succeed. But for athletes like boxers, the aggression is a bit more obvious.

Golfers are aggressive towards a ball, so they can hit it a long way.

Tennis players may hit the ball very hard towards their opponent.

Boxers actually try to harm their opponent.

Aggression in sport must be controlled, otherwise it can make your performance worse.

Learn about aggression — LEARN IT OR ELSE!

You'll need to learn the kinds of things that introverts and extroverts prefer — time to cover the page again and see how much of it you can write down. Pick a couple of friends, an introvert and an extrovert — associate the different qualities with them. It makes it a bit more relevant to you.

Section Two — Health and Fitness

Hygiene

Hygiene's pretty important. Without it, the world would be a dirtier, smellier, yuckier place. So you need to know what to keep clean, and what happens if you let it get smelly.

Hygiene Helps Keep You Healthy and Odour-Free

This is important for keeping yourself healthy, and also for staying popular with your friends. Your hygiene routine should include paying attention to:

WASHING:
Have a regular shower or bath and dry yourself properly to avoid dirt and grime building up, B.O. (Body Odour), and infections.

TEETH:
Brush your teeth at least twice a day, and get them checked over regularly by a dentist to avoid tooth decay, gum disease and dog breath — especially as you get older.

CLOTHES:
Change your clothes often, and especially after playing sport, to avoid whiffy smells.

SWEAT
1) When you exercise, your body produces sweat to help keep you cool.
2) Sweat is a mixture of water, salts, ammonia, and other waste products.
3) Sweat itself doesn't smell, but when bacteria on your skin start feeding on it, they start to get pretty whiffy.

I've been eating sweat again.

Avoid Athlete's Foot and Verrucas by wearing Flip-Flops

Athlete's foot and verrucas are infections you can easily catch, but just as easily avoid.

ATHLETE'S FOOT:
1) It's a fungus that grows between your toes and makes them itch.
2) You catch it through contact with infected socks, towels or changing room floors.
3) Avoid it by wearing flip-flops in shared changing rooms, always drying between your toes after washing them, and avoiding shoes or socks that make your feet sweat.
4) It can be treated with powder or ointment from the chemist.

Athlete's foot is a fungus between your toes.

VERRUCAS:
1) These are flat warts that grow on the bottom of your feet.
2) They're very easily caught — and are transmitted in the same way as athlete's foot.
3) Always wear flip-flops when sharing a changing room with other people.
4) They can be treated with ointment or pads from the chemist.

Hurrah for flip-flops.

Bad Shoes Mean Bad Feet

Ill-fitting shoes can give your feet no end of trouble...

BLISTERS:
1) These are usually caused by shoes which rub.
2) Don't burst a blister — it increases the risk of infection.
3) If it bursts on its own, keep it clean and dry.

BUNIONS:
1) A bunion is an inflammation of the joint between your big toe and your foot.
2) Only surgery can get rid of these.

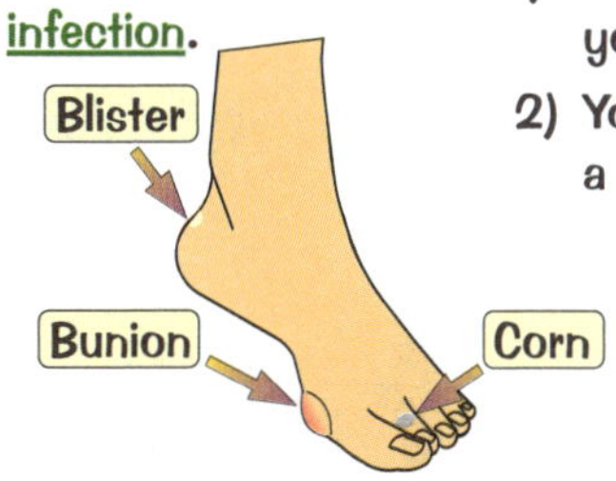

CORNS:
1) These are hard pads of skin on your toes and feet.
2) You can get corn plasters from a chemist to get rid of them.

Blister, Bunion, Corn

The BBC of ill-fitting shoes: Blisters, Bunions & Corns

Corn you believe it? It's odour this world...

Not too much on this page really. Make sure you know some important points for a hygiene routine, and extra sure you know how to avoid athlete's foot and verrucas. And if anyone asks you what damage badly fitting shoes can cause — just think BBC, for blisters, bunions and corns.

Section Two — Health and Fitness

Drugs

Doping, or taking drugs, is a big problem in sport. You'll need to know the different kinds of drugs that can be taken, what they do, and why they're banned in international competitions.

Alcohol and Tobacco are Legal but Harmful

Although alcohol and tobacco are legal, they're still drugs and can affect your performance badly.

ALCOHOL:
1) Affects your coordination, speech and judgement.
2) Slows your reactions.
3) Makes your muscles get tired more quickly.
4) Eventually damages your liver, kidneys, heart, muscles, brain, and the digestive and immune systems.

SMOKING:
1) Causes nose, throat and chest irritations.
2) Makes you short of breath.
3) Increases the risk of developing heart disease, lung cancer, bronchitis, and other diseases.

Small amounts of alcohol don't do too much harm, but every cigarette does damage.

Performance Enhancing Drugs — Remember SNAPD

These performance enhancing drugs are banned by the International Olympic Committee (IOC).

STIMULANTS
1) Speed up your reactions and increase aggression.
2) Make you feel less pain.

But...
1) Feeling less pain can make an athlete train too hard.
2) They can lead to high blood pressure, heart and liver problems, and strokes.
3) They're addictive.

NARCOTIC ANALGESICS
1) Kill pain — so injuries and fatigue don't affect performance so much.

But...
1) They're addictive, with unpleasant withdrawal symptoms.
2) Feeling less pain can make an athlete train too hard.
3) They can lead to constipation and low blood pressure.

An easy way to remember which drugs are banned by the IOC is to remember SNAPD.

S — Stimulants
N — Narcotic analgesics
A — Anabolic agents
P — Peptide hormones
D — Diuretics

ANABOLIC AGENTS
(or steroids)
1) Increase muscle size.
2) Allow athletes to train harder.

But...
1) They cause high blood pressure, heart disease, infertility and cancer.
2) Women may grow facial and body hair, and their voice may deepen.

PEPTIDE HORMONES
1) Most have a similar effect to anabolic steroids.
2) EPO (Erythropoietin) has a similar effect to blood doping (see next page).

But...
They can cause strokes and abnormal growth.

DIURETICS
1) Make you urinate, causing weight loss — important if you're competing in a certain weight division.
2) Can mask traces of other drugs in the body.

But...
They can cause cramp and dehydration.

A lot of these drugs were developed as medicines — but misuse does damage.

Anna Bolic — Don't mess with her...

Remember that alcohol generally makes you do everything more slowly — speak, react, think etc. And make sure you can write down what each of the different kinds of drug actually do.

Section Two — Health and Fitness

Drugs

People cheat in sport by taking banned or restricted drugs. Fortunately, there are drug testing procedures with severe punishments so they won't get away with it. And you've gotta know 'em.

B CALM Drugs are Restricted

The International Olympic Committee (IOC) restricts the use of these drugs — learn what they are.

BETA BLOCKERS
1) They're medicines that lower the heart rate, steady shaking hands and reduce anxiety.
2) They're banned in sports where they might give an advantage, such as shooting, ski-jumping, snooker and bobsleigh.

CORTICOSTEROIDS
1) They help reduce pain and inflammation from injuries.
2) They have some quite serious side effects, including diabetes, depression and bone weakness.

To remember the restricted drugs, remember B CALM.

B — Beta blockers
C — Corticosteroids
A — Alcohol
L — Local anaesthetics
M — Marijuana

ALCOHOL
It's sometimes used in snooker or shooting to calm nerves.

LOCAL ANAESTHETICS
They reduce pain, but might be allowed for medical purposes.

MARIJUANA
It has a similar effect to alcohol.

Dope Testing can happen at Any Time

There are strict procedures for drug testing. They protect athletes and mean results can be double-checked. If an athlete is found guilty, punishments can be severe — including lifetime bans.

THE TESTING PROCEDURE:
1) Urine samples are divided into two bottles — the A- and B-samples.
2) The A-sample is tested. If drugs are found, the B-sample is tested to double-check the result.
3) Refusing to give a sample is as serious as failing a drugs test.

PUNISHMENTS FOR CHEATS:
If an athlete is found guilty of taking banned drugs, they're banned from competing — possibly forever.

All of the testing takes place in official labs — and no one is supposed to know whose sample they're testing.

Athletes can be tested at any time.

Can't you wait until I finish?

Blood Doping is Banned

Blood doping and 'physical manipulation' are also banned, since athletes get an unfair advantage.

BLOOD DOPING:
Blood doping is used to simulate high-altitude training — without actually going to high altitude.
1) Red blood cells are taken out of an athlete — their body then makes more red blood cells to replace them.
2) Before a competition, the red blood cells are injected back, so that more oxygen can be carried round their body.

Possible side effects include allergic reactions, kidney damage, viruses (such as AIDS), and blocked capillaries.

PHYSICAL MANIPULATION:
This includes interfering with a urine sample after it's been given.

DRUG TESTING LABORATORY

"Urine Safe Hands"

Just our little motto.

B CALM — the exam's easy if you know this...

Make extra sure you know the difference between the B CALM drugs on this page and the SNAPD drugs on the previous page — SNAPD drugs are banned, but B CALM drugs are restricted. Also be sure to learn why urine samples are split into A- and B- samples — it's so they can check results.

Section Two — Health and Fitness

Other Things that Affect Performance

There are also some other things that can affect your performance. They're not all things you can control — but they are all things you have to know about before you go into your exam.

Physiological Factors Affect Your Body

Things like lack of sleep or a cold can also affect performance. Be sure you know about these.

ILLNESS OR MEDICAL CONDITION:
1) Colds or flu can make you short of breath, affect your concentration, and make you feel weak.
2) Asthma affects the breathing, but can be controlled.
3) Hayfever is an allergy to pollen from plants. It causes sneezing, and makes your eyes water and your nose run.
4) Anaemia is when you don't have enough red blood cells — or your red blood cells don't have enough haemoglobin. It can make you short of breath and dizzy.

STALENESS:
Poor form and staleness can be caused by overdoing things — like exercising without enough breaks.

FATIGUE:
When your body hasn't had time to recover from exercise, your performance can be affected.

LACK OF SLEEP:
Without enough sleep, you lose strength and concentration more quickly.

MENSTRUATION:
Women seem to perform better at certain stages of the menstrual cycle.

I'm ready.

ABC is for Agility, Balance and Coordination

These factors can also affect performance. They're important — so you need to learn them.

AGILITY:
When you can change direction and body position very quickly.

BALANCE: When you don't wobble or fall over easily.

COORDINATION: When you can move your body precisely and smoothly to respond to something.

Other Factors can have an Effect

ENVIRONMENT/WEATHER/CLIMATE:
1) Hot or humid weather can adversely affect your performance in a lot of sports e.g. running, tennis.
2) In the same way, if it's freezing cold or very windy, you're likely to play many sports worse.

SENSES:
Sharp eyesight or a delicate sense of touch can be important.

EQUIPMENT:
The better your equipment, the better you're likely to perform.

MENTAL ABILITY:
When you play sport, you have to make good decisions. A lot of it comes down to practice.

TECHNOLOGY:
Technological developments in equipment, materials and training methods (e.g. using video and computer technology) are pushing back the bounds of performance.

EXPERIENCE:
This is often vital in competitions.

MENTAL PREPARATION:
Relaxation techniques can reduce anxiety and help performers focus on the task at hand. Mental rehearsal will also help preparation.

PHYSICAL ABILITY:
This is your fitness and skill level. You need to learn skills and practise to improve them and to keep fit.

ALTITUDE:
People who live or train at high altitude perform better in many endurance events.

Experience can be vital (in competitions).

Sporty lake monster — fit-ness...

You can remember the physiological factors that affect your performance by remembering FILMS — and how about STAMP MEEE for those 'other factors'. Whatever you do though, keep a note of all these memory aids — and make sure you know what they're helping you to remember.

Section Two — Health and Fitness

Revision Summary for Section Two

That's it then — the end of another section. There's lots in it, but it's all stuff you need to know for the exam. You'll need to learn all the info about fitness — what it is and how things like diet, age, drugs and so on can affect it. Then there are the bits about health and hygiene. But don't panic — all you need to do is learn the facts, and then the exam will be easy. To test how much you know, and how much you still need to revise, try these questions — and keep revising until you know all the answers.

1) Name seven factors that can affect someone's health.
2) Give a definition of general fitness.
3) As well as being generally fit, what six things do you need for specific fitness?
4) Name six factors that can affect fitness.
5) Name three types of people who should take things easy when they start to exercise.
6) Give two examples of how you can get more exercise by changing bad habits.
7) What changes 'kick in' when you start to exercise to keep your muscles supplied with oxygen?
8) What substance is responsible for these changes, and what type of substance is it?
9) What does 'shunting blood' mean?
10) What does your body do to cool you down when exercising?
11) Why do you still need lots of oxygen after you've finished exercising hard?
12) Describe the benefits of aerobic training.
13) What is hypertrophy?
14) About what percentage of your calories should be proteins? Carbohydrates? Fats? What other nutrients do you need?
15) What are the two kinds of amino acids? What are the two kinds of carbohydrates? And the three kinds of fats?
16) Why do you need water-soluble vitamins regularly?
17) Why is having the right amount of water in your body so important? How does your body control your water balance?
18) Why is fibre so funky?
19) Describe what is meant by a balanced diet.
20) What are the two things you should do if you want to lose weight?
21) Name the two ways in which glucose can be converted into energy. When is each way used?
22) What are the three kinds of strength? What's the difference between strength and power?
23) Why is flexibility important for sport? How could you improve your flexibility?
24) Name six ways in which age can affect performance at sport. How does gender affect performance?
25) Name the three basic somatotypes. How would you describe each of these somatotypes? Give an example of a sport that each somatotype is suited to.
26) Which kinds of sports do introverts and extroverts usually prefer?
27) Name three things you should definitely include in your hygiene routine.
28) What is athlete's foot? And what's a verruca? How would you avoid them?
29) Name three foot problems that you can get if your shoes don't fit properly.
30) What five kinds of drugs are banned by the IOC? What five kinds are restricted?
31) What is blood doping?
32) Name five physiological factors that can affect somebody's performance at sport.
33) Name 12 other factors that can affect performance (yes, 12, a dozen, douze, zwölf, doce).

Section Two — Health and Fitness

Section Three — Training & Sporting Skills

Training Sessions

Training's not about running for as long as possible, or lifting the heaviest weights you can. There's much more to it than that — and you'll be asked about it in the exam, so get reading.

Always Warm Up First and Cool Down Afterwards

These are vital to every training session — make sure you know why:

WARM-UP — gradually gets your body ready for the training.
1) Increases the temperature of the body, and increases blood flow to the muscles — so they can do the work later on in the training.
2) Stretches the muscles, moves the joints and increases the range of movement — so you're ready for the work and less likely to injure yourself.
3) Concentrates the mind on the training.

COOL-DOWN — gets your body back to normal.
1) Helps replace the oxygen debt in your muscles, and so gets rid of any lactic acid which could cause stiffness later.
2) Gets rid of the extra blood in your muscles, and so stops it pooling in your veins. Blood pooling can make you feel dizzy and weak if you stop exercising suddenly.

Training should be Interesting as well as Useful

TRAINING — An exercise routine needs these three things to make it interesting and useful:
1) Loads of different things in each session — so you don't get bored.
2) Time to warm up and cool down.
3) Regular checking and assessment to make sure it's still suitable and good enough.

SPOR — The Four Principles of Training

S → SPECIFICITY — Every person will need a different training program — we're all different and we all do different things.
  1) Train the right parts of the body — there's no point making a weightlifter run 10 miles a day — it won't improve their weightlifting.
  2) Train to the right level — if someone's dead unfit, don't start them with a 5-mile swim.

P → PROGRESSION — Steadily increase the amount of training that's done — but only when the body has adapted to the previous training.

O → OVERLOAD — You've got to make your body work harder than it normally would. You've got to push yourself beyond the training threshold. It's the only way to get fitter. You can overload by increasing any of these three:
  1) Frequency of training (e.g. training more often),
  2) Intensity of training (e.g. lifting heavier weights),
  3) Duration of training (e.g. training for 5 minutes longer each session).

R → REVERSIBILITY — Your fitness level changes all the time — and it will go down if you stop training. It takes much longer to gain fitness than to lose fitness, which is a pain in the bum if you ask me.

SPOR — the Greek God of mushroom reproduction...

Warming up and cooling down is pretty obvious, and just needs learning. The same goes for ways to make training interesting. But the principles of training are much harder. Just remember that the four principles begin with the first four letters of 'sport': SPOR. That might help a bit...

Training Sessions

The best training programmes aren't just thrown together at the last moment — they have to be <u>carefully</u> planned. All the stuff you need to know is here — get it all in your head.

A <u>Training Programme</u> must <u>Suit</u> the Person it's for

The programme must <u>suit the person it's for</u> — so you've got to find out about them.
Good questions to ask them include...

- What exercise do you like?
- How fit are you now?
- What sports do you play?
- How old are you?
- Do you have any injuries?
- Do you have any health problems?
- What exercise do you find boring?
- Do you live near any sports facilities?
- Why do you want to get fitter?

I'm begging you — no more questions.

There are <u>Four Stages</u> of Training for <u>Competition</u>

Your training should be different for each stage of the year.
1) <u>Out-of-season preparation</u> — Eat plenty of carbohydrates, and do lots of aerobic and strength training.
2) <u>Pre-season preparation</u> — Do anaerobic, aerobic and skills training — plus some extra strength training.
3) <u>Competition</u> — Compete regularly, while maintaining your fitness and getting enough rest. Training can be planned so that you '<u>peak</u>' at the right time (e.g. for key competitions).
4) <u>Recuperation</u> — Recover from the strain of competition through rest and relaxation.

Programmes can be Planned using <u>FITT</u>

<u>F</u> = <u>FREQUENCY</u> of activity — how <u>often</u> you should exercise.
E.g. if you just want to stay healthy you should exercise for at least 20 minutes twice a week. If you do a hard workout you should give your body at least <u>24 hours rest</u> before you exercise again.

Remember to give yourself 24 hours rest after every hard exercise session.

I think I might have overdone it.

<u>I</u> = <u>INTENSITY</u> of activity — how <u>hard</u> you should exercise.
E.g. if you wanted to <u>lose weight</u> you should raise your heart rate to about 75% of your maximum safe heart rate for 20 minutes or over. (<u>Max heart rate</u> is about 220 minus your age in years.) The level of intensity at which training improves physical fitness is called the <u>training threshold</u>.

<u>T</u> = <u>TIME</u> of activity — how <u>long</u> you should exercise.
<u>Aerobic</u> training sessions tend to last for <u>20 minutes</u> or longer.
<u>Strength</u> training sessions are generally shorter and less sustained.

I've been hula-hooping for fifty years.

Maybe the desert wasn't the best place to go snorkelling...

<u>T</u> = <u>TYPE</u> of activity — <u>what exercises</u> you should use.
It can be good to <u>vary</u> training sessions to stop you tiring of the same old workout. When applied to aerobic training this is called <u>cross training</u> — a different exercise (e.g. cycling instead of running) is used to <u>increase fitness</u>, but <u>without over-stressing</u> the tissues and joints used in the main sport.

<u>Climatic conditions</u> can also affect the type of exercise — e.g. they can make training for some sports difficult in <u>winter</u>. One solution is to travel abroad for <u>warm weather</u> or <u>altitude training</u> — but of course this depends on having the necessary <u>funds</u> or <u>sponsorship</u>.

What's yellow and swings from tree to tree? *answer on page 34*

Use <u>FITT</u> to get fit — <u>F</u>requency, <u>I</u>ntensity, <u>T</u>ime and <u>T</u>ype. Remember that the training has got to be suited to the <u>individual</u> — it's no good making an unfit businessman run 10 miles a day in his first week of training. And make sure that the training's not too <u>boring</u>, or you'll never do any...

Section Three — Training and Sporting Skills

Training Methods

There's more to weight training than just pumping iron — you've got to grunt as well... Oh yes and there are all these different ways of increasing strength too — with flippin' silly names...

Weight Training improves Muscle Strength and Tone

There are three kinds of strength:
1) Explosive strength — e.g. discus, shot-put.
2) Static strength — e.g. holding up a heavy weight.
3) Dynamic strength — e.g. moving a heavy object.

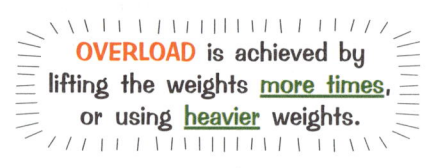

OVERLOAD is achieved by lifting the weights more times, or using heavier weights.

There are two kinds of weight training you need to know about: Isometric and isotonic training.

Isometric Training —
Muscles Contract, but there's No Movement

ADVANTAGES:
1) Develops strength — especially static strength.
2) Cheap, quick and easy to do anywhere.

*EXAMPLE: THE WALL SIT
Sit with your back to the wall and your knees bent at 90° and hold it.*

DISADVANTAGES:
1) Muscles gain most strength at the angle used in exercise.
2) Not good if you've got heart problems — blood flow to the muscle is reduced during exercise, so the blood pressure rises, putting more strain on the heart for little improvement in fitness.

Isotonic Training —
Muscles Contract and Shorten producing Movement

ADVANTAGES:
1) Strengthens the muscle throughout the range of movement.
2) Easily adaptable to suit most sports.

*EXAMPLE: PULL-UPS
Hang from a bar and then pull yourself up until your head is over it.*

DISADVANTAGES:
1) Muscles can become sore because of the stress they're under when lengthening.
2) Muscles gain the most strength when they're at their weakest point of action.

Pressure Training Simulates the Pressure of Competition

The idea here is to increase the pressure on the player when training. Ways to increase the pressure include:
1) 'One shot' — in which only a single shot or attempt is allowed.
2) Using visualisation to imagine that you're in an important competition.
3) Scoring methods — scores are given to practice performances, and either the performances or the players in a team are ranked.

ADVANTAGES:
1) Pressure training means you're more likely to cope with the pressure of a real competition.
2) It's especially useful for high-pressure games — e.g. tennis, or team sports like football.

GET IT IN! OR ELSE...

DISADVANTAGES:
1) The training can be less enjoyable.
2) It's not so much use to amateurs.

Isovindaloo training — go for the burn...

So you want muscles like Arnie...? Well, this is the topic that'll tell you how to do it — kind of. But never mind what you want, the examiners will want you to be able to churn out all the major points that are mentioned on these two pages. You know the drill — cover up the page and get scribbling...

Section Three — Training and Sporting Skills

Training Methods

These methods can all be used to increase <u>endurance</u> — and circuit training's good for <u>strength</u> too.

Circuit Training uses loads of Different Exercises

Each circuit has between 8 and 15 stations in it. At each station you do a specific exercise for a set amount of time before moving onto the next station. You're allowed a short rest between stations.

ADVANTAGES:
1) <u>Less boring</u> because the exercises are all different.
2) Easily <u>adaptable</u> (can be done indoors and outdoors).
3) It can include <u>weight training</u> and <u>aerobic</u> exercise.

DISADVANTAGES:
1) Can be a <u>pain</u> to set up.
2) People can get in each other's way if the circuit is <u>busy</u>.

OVERLOAD is achieved by doing <u>more repetitions</u> at each station, by completing the circuit <u>more quickly</u>, <u>resting less</u> between stations, or by repeating the circuit.

Continuous Training means No Resting

<u>Continuous training</u> involves exercising at a <u>constant rate</u> doing activities like running or cycling. It usually means exercising at <u>60-90% of VO$_2$ Max</u> for an <u>hour</u> or more. When done at the lower end of this range, it is often referred to as <u>long, slow distance training</u> — or <u>LSD</u> for short.

ADVANTAGES:
1) Needs only a <u>small amount</u> of <u>easy-to-use</u> equipment.
2) Good for <u>aerobic fitness</u> and using up <u>body fat</u>.

DISADVANTAGES:
1) Can be really <u>boring</u>.
2) <u>Doesn't</u> improve sprinting, so not ideal for many games, like football and hockey.

OVERLOAD is achieved by increasing the duration, distance, speed, or frequency of training.

After six years of continuous training surely I deserve a rest...

Fartlek Training is all about Changes of Speed

<u>Fartlek training</u> can be made easy or hard to suit your fitness. Fartlek training can be adapted to fit any continuous exercise (e.g. running, cycling, swimming, rowing). It involves changes in <u>intensity</u> and type of exercise <u>without stopping</u>. For example, part of a fartlek run could be to sprint for 10 seconds, then jog for 20 seconds (repeated for 4 minutes) — followed by long-stride running for 2 minutes.

ADVANTAGES:
1) Good for sports that need <u>different paces</u>, like football and basketball.
2) <u>Easily changed</u> to suit an individual or a particular sport.

DISADVANTAGES:
1) <u>Difficult</u> to see how hard the person is training.
2) Too easy to <u>skip</u> the hard bits if you can't be bothered.

OVERLOAD is achieved by increasing the times or speeds of each bit, or the terrain difficulty (e.g. running uphill).

Interval Training uses Fixed Patterns of Exercise

<u>Fixed patterns</u> of fast and slow exercise are used in interval training. Each repetition of a pattern is called a '<u>rep</u>' (repetition), and you've got to finish a '<u>set</u>' (group of reps) before a rest.

ADVANTAGES:
1) Can <u>mix</u> aerobic and anaerobic exercise.
2) Easy to see when an athlete <u>isn't trying</u>.

DISADVANTAGES:
1) Hard to <u>keep going</u>.
2) A bit <u>dull</u>.

OVERLOAD is achieved by increasing the reps or sets. Or by spending less time resting inbetween sets.

Fartlek training .... (Add your own joke.)

This section on training methods doesn't mess around — everything does exactly what it says in the <u>heading</u>. So it's not difficult — but it's loads more boring <u>lists</u> to learn. Oh, and in case you were wondering, <u>fartlek</u> actually means '<u>speed play</u>' in Swedish. How disappointing...

Section Three — Training and Sporting Skills

Aerobic Fitness Testing

You've got to know what aerobic fitness is, how to measure it and how to improve it.

It's Good to have a High Aerobic Fitness Level

If you've got a high aerobic fitness level, it should mean that compared with people of average fitness:
1) Your heart rate will be lower when resting, and when exercising.
2) You can exercise for longer without feeling tired.
3) You can use up more oxygen when you're exercising.

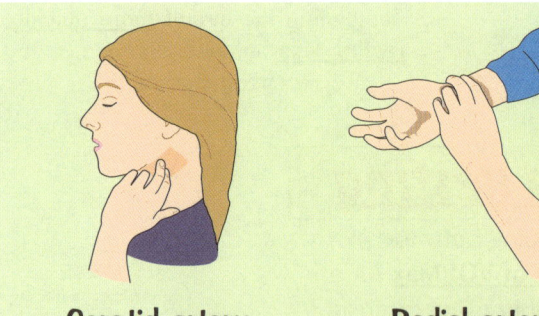

MEASURING YOUR HEART RATE
Put your first two fingers on one of these two pulse points:
1) Carotid artery — on your neck, to the side of the lumpy bit in the middle.
2) Radial artery — that's on your wrist, by the base of your thumb.

Count the beats over fifteen seconds (e.g. 17). Times that number by four (17 X 4 = 68) to get your beats per minute — that's your heart rate (heart rate is 68 beats per minute).

Carotid artery   Radial artery

There are Three Main Tests for Aerobic Fitness

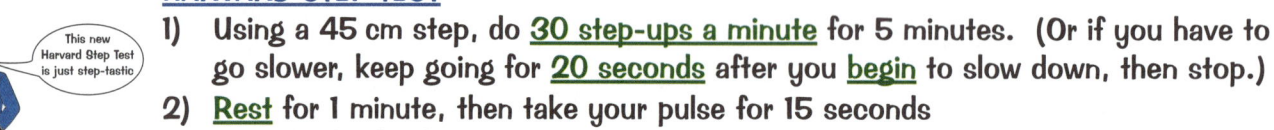

HARVARD STEP TEST

This new Harvard Step Test is just step-tastic

1) Using a 45 cm step, do 30 step-ups a minute for 5 minutes. (Or if you have to go slower, keep going for 20 seconds after you begin to slow down, then stop.)
2) Rest for 1 minute, then take your pulse for 15 seconds — multiply this by 4 to get your heart rate.
3) Use this formula to work out your score — the higher your score, the fitter you are.

$$\frac{\text{length of exercise in seconds} \times 100}{5.5 \times \text{pulse count}}$$

4) There are different versions of the Harvard step test so check the details (height of the step, rest time etc.) before comparing results.

12-MINUTE RUN
1) Jog to warm up.
2) When a whistle sounds, run round a track as many times as you can in 12 minutes.
3) The distance you ran is recorded. The further you can run, the fitter you are.

MULTISTAGE FITNESS TEST
1) You must run 'shuttles' between 2 lines, 20 metres apart. Start on the first bleep.
2) Your foot must be on or over the next line when the next bleep sounds.
3) The time between bleeps gets shorter, so you have to run faster.
4) If you miss a beep you are allowed two further beeps to catch up. If you miss three beeps in a row, the level and number of shuttles completed are noted as your final score.
5) Your Maximal Oxygen Consumption can then be calculated.
6) The higher your Maximal Oxygen Consumption (VO_2max), the fitter you are.

Tarzypan!

Fitness is a dead important part of PE — everyone knows that. But you've got to know how to test for aerobic fitness. Make sure you learn how to take your pulse including the names of the arteries. If you don't kill yourself trying out the Cooper test learn the three tests in all their glory.

Section Three — Training and Sporting Skills

Fitness Testing

Aerobic fitness isn't the only thing you'll need to know how to test. You've also got to know about testing muscular endurance, strength and flexibility. Here's the info — get learning.

There are Different Tests for Different Types of Fitness

Fitness isn't just how long you can run for or how much you can lift. Overall fitness includes endurance, strength, power, agility and flexibilty — you can measure each with a different test.

ENDURANCE TESTING
Test the endurance of different muscles by seeing how many times you can do an exercise — e.g. sit-ups or press-ups.

BALANCE TESTING — THE STORK STAND TEST
Stand on your best leg with your other foot touching your knee, eyes closed and your hands on your hips. Time how long you can stand there. Wobbling's allowed, but no moving your feet or hands, or opening your eyes. Take the best of three times.

AGILITY TESTING
Test agility by setting up any kind of course that means changing direction frequently and timing the run.

SPEED TESTING
Any test that involves moving fast over a short distance will be good for this. E.g. the sprint test — simply time how long it takes you to run 100 m.

STRENGTH TESTING
This kind of dynamometer measures hand and forearm strength.

Just grip as hard as you can...

Any test longer than 30 seconds isn't a good strength test — it's better for testing muscular endurance.

Cheat!

A dynamometer's probably the best way to measure strength...

A course involving lots of changes of direction is a good test of agility.

You Have to Stretch to Test Flexibility

There are loads of different ways to test flexibility — but most of them just measure how far you can stretch. You do different stretches to measure different parts of the body.

SHOULDER LIFT TEST
This measures flexibility at the shoulders.
1) Lie face down on the floor.
2) Grab a 50 cm stick with both hands, keeping your hands shoulder width apart.
3) Raise the stick with straight arms — but keep your chin on the floor.
4) Measure how far you can raise the stick off the floor.

Move stick this way
Keep chin on ground.

The higher you can lift the stick, the more supple you are.

Ruler

SIT AND REACH TEST
This measures flexibility in the back and lower hamstrings.
1) Sit on the floor with your legs pointing straight out in front of you.
2) Push a ruler, placed on a box, as far forwards as you can with your fingers — keeping your legs straight all the time.

Learn this page — and give your brain a stretch...

Just like you get tested on how much you know about PE, athletes get tested on things like muscle strength, endurance and their flexibility — so you've got to know how to test them. There's not that much you can learn about a dynamometer, but make sure you know the sit and reach test really well.

Section Three — Training and Sporting Skills

Sporting Injuries

There's two different types of injury that you can get from playing sport — chronic and acute injuries.

Chronic Injuries are Caused by Overuse

CHRONIC INJURIES — caused by continuous stress on part of the body over a long period of time:
1) Tennis players can develop tennis elbow — painful inflammation of tendons in the elbow due to overuse of certain arm muscles.
2) Golfers get a similar chronic injury called, wait for it... golfer's elbow.
3) Long-distance runners can develop a nasty bone injury in the leg called shin splints.
4) You're at risk of a chronic injury if you train too hard, don't rest enough between training sessions, use poor footwear, or have bad technique.

Acute Injuries are Caused by a Sudden Stress

ACUTE INJURIES — happen when there's a sudden stress on the body. They come in all sorts of nasty forms, like bone fractures, pulled muscles, and concussion — and they're caused by things like:

1) Colliding with an opponent or obstacle, e.g. in sports like rugby and football.
2) Being hit by something, e.g. a cricket ball, squash racket or boxing glove.
3) Falling a) from a height, e.g. in rock-climbing, mountaineering or skiing.
   b) at high speed, e.g. in skiing, cycling, horse racing or running.

A Lot of Injuries can be Prevented

BEFORE THE GAME:
1) Take off anything that could get caught (e.g. jewellery, watches).
2) Use the right equipment — and check it's in good condition.
3) Watch out for possible dangers in the playing environment, e.g. stones or glass hidden in grass, or slippery patches caused by bad weather.
4) Use the correct technique, including when lifting/carrying/placing equipment.
5) Warm up before the activity, making sure you exercise the muscles you're going to use.

Officials help to make sure there's fair play...

DURING THE GAME:
1) Play with people of a similar size, strength and skill level.
2) Know and follow the rules of the game.
3) Use the correct technique.
4) Wear suitable footwear (e.g. studded football boots, spiked running shoes).
5) Use protective clothing/equipment where appropriate (e.g. padding in cricket, cycling helmet).
6) Use officials (e.g. a referee) to ensure there's fair play and to make sure that the rules are followed.

AFTERWARDS:
1) Cool down properly.
2) Give yourself plenty of time to recover before playing again.

Not guilty — the sporting verdict in juries...

This is the kind of topic where you just need to learn plenty of examples to reel off in the exam. For both injury types (sudden and continuous stress), think of places and events where they're most likely to happen. And think of different injuries for each type. The stuff on preventing injuries will give you ideas for examples too — so make sure you've memorised all the points.

Section Three — Training and Sporting Skills

Sporting Injuries

Injuries are also categorised as soft tissue or hard tissue injuries. It's simple enough — hard tissue injuries are when the bone is damaged, and soft tissue injuries are all the others.

Most Sporting Injuries are to Soft Tissue

OPEN INJURIES:
Open injuries are where the skin's broken, usually letting blood escape. They're things like cuts, grazes, blisters and chafing.

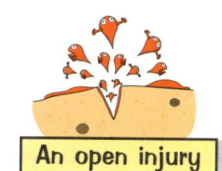

An open injury

Oh look — a closed injury.

CLOSED INJURIES:
Closed injuries happen beneath the skin — there's no external bleeding.

1) Bruising is when your blood vessels get damaged — you bleed inside.

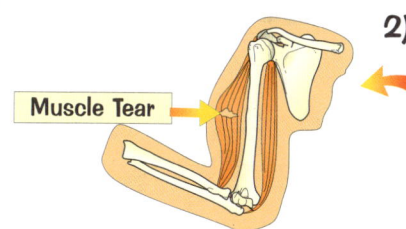

2) Strained (pulled) muscles and tendons are tears in the tissue — they're caused by sudden overstretching. Pulled hamstrings and calf muscles are common injuries in loads of sports like football and cricket.

Muscle Tear

3) Sprains are joint injuries where the ligament has been stretched or torn, usually because of violent twisting.

4) Joints can get dislocated as well. The bone is pulled out of its normal position — again, it's twisting that usually does it.

Dislocated shoulder — Humerus pulled out of joint.

5) Cartilage can also be damaged. E.g. the cartilage of the knee can be torn by a violent impact or twisting motion. This injury is common in sports like football.

Hard Tissue Injuries are Bone Fractures

Fractures are either cracks in the bone or an actual break. All hard tissue injuries are bone fractures. Just like with soft tissue injuries, they can be open or closed.

1) Fractures are usually accompanied by bruising and swelling. This is because they damage blood vessels in or around the bone.

2) They'll also cause a lot of pain because of the damaged nerves inside the bone.

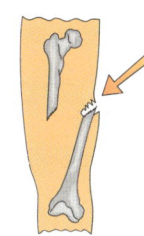

In an open fracture the skin is torn and the bone pokes out. Urgghh.

In a closed fracture it all happens under the skin. The skin itself is alright.

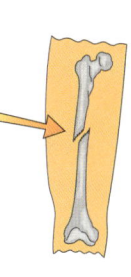

STRESS FRACTURES
A 'stress fracture' is a crack along the length of a bone. It's caused by continuous stress over a long period of time (so it's a chronic injury). All other bone fractures are acute injuries. Long-distance runners get stress fractures called shin splints.

Hard tissue! — Bless you — A soft tissue, please...

If the skin's broken it's an open injury, otherwise it's closed — that's easy enough to remember. Make sure you can recall every injury mentioned here, describe what it is, and give examples of where it happens. And remember, sprains are a bit like strains but they happen at the joints.

Section Three — Training and Sporting Skills

Injury — Types and Treatment

And here's some more lovely stuff on injuries and treating them. Enjoy...

Severe Environments can cause Serious Conditions

Hyperthermia
SYMPTOMS: Body temperature gets too high — weak pulse, clammy pale skin. Results from over-exercising and dehydration (lack of water), especially on a hot day. Long-distance runners and cyclists are particularly at risk.
TREATMENT: Lay the patient down in a cool place, and give them liquids. Get advice from a doctor.

Hypothermia
SYMPTOMS: Body temperature falls below 35 °C. Muscles go rigid, heart beats irregularly, casualty may fall unconscious.
TREATMENT: Steadily raise body temperature to 37 °C. Put them into warm, dry clothing or wrap them in a blanket. Give them hot drinks, and maybe a warm bath.

Cramp, Concussion, Stitch — other Common Problems

Cramp
SYMPTOMS: Involuntary contraction of a muscle caused by lack of salt minerals in the blood, or by lack of blood flowing to a muscle. It's painful, but easy to treat.
TREATMENT: Just stretch the muscle and hold it like that, massaging it gently, until the muscle relaxes.

Winding
SYMPTOMS: Difficulty in breathing, pain in the abdomen, and might feel sick. Caused by a blow to the abdomen.
TREATMENT: Stop exercising, lean forward, and rub the affected area.

Shock
SYMPTOMS: Pale, clammy skin. Rapid, weak pulse and breathing. May feel weak, faint, sick, dizzy or thirsty. Caused by a drop in blood pressure.
TREATMENT: Call an ambulance, stem any external bleeding, reassure them, place in recovery position.

Concussion
SYMPTOMS: Unconsciousness, disorientation, memory loss. Caused by a blow to the head.
TREATMENT: If unconscious, place in the recovery position (see next page) and get an ambulance. If conscious, keep casualty under observation for 24 hours.

Stitch
SYMPTOMS: A sharp pain in your side or abdomen. It's basically cramp of the diaphragm and can make breathing difficult. Caused by vigorous exercise too soon after eating.
TREATMENT: Stop exercising, take deep breaths, and breathe out slowly.

Ow — I've got cramp in my leg.

The RICE Method treats Minor Soft Tissue Injuries

The RICE method is a good treatment for soft tissue injuries like sprains, strains or bruises. It reduces pain, swelling and bruising. But don't use it if you think there may be a fracture. It's sometimes just known as ICE (well, the 'R' bit is pretty obvious).

R — REST ➡ Stop immediately and rest the injury — if you carry on, you'll make it worse.

I — ICE ➡ Apply ice to the injury. This makes the blood vessels contract to reduce internal bleeding and swelling.

C — COMPRESSION ➡ Bandaging the injury will also help reduce swelling. But don't make it so tight that you stop the blood circulating altogether.

E — ELEVATION ➡ Support the limb at a raised level (i.e. above the heart). The flow of blood reduces because it has to flow against gravity.

I've got the rice.
What are they doing?

If the RICE treatment doesn't work, try noodles...

Well, it goes without saying that you need to learn everything on this page. For each condition or injury, practise scribbling down the symptoms and the treatments until you're getting them all right. The RICE method is really important — you've got to know when to use and when not to use it.

Section Three — Training and Sporting Skills

Injury — Types and Treatment

The DRABC first aid treatment is for serious injuries where the casualty seems to be unconscious. DRABC stands for Danger, Response, Airway, Breathing, Circulation — the things to check first.

Use DRABC if they seem to be Unconscious

D — Check for any immediate DANGER
1) Make sure there's no danger to you or the casualty.
2) Clear the surrounding area, and stop any games.

R — Check for a RESPONSE
1) Check if they're conscious. Ask if they can hear you. If not, gently shake them to see if they respond.
2) If they're unconscious, continue with ABC.

A — Make sure the AIRWAY is clear
1) Tilt the head back.
2) Check the tongue's not blocking the airway.
3) Loosen tight clothing. Clear away any vomit.

B — Look for signs of BREATHING
1) Look at their chest to see if it's moving.
2) Put your cheek by their mouth — try to feel their breath.

C — Check for CIRCULATION
Feel the neck to see if the casualty has a pulse (carotid pulse).

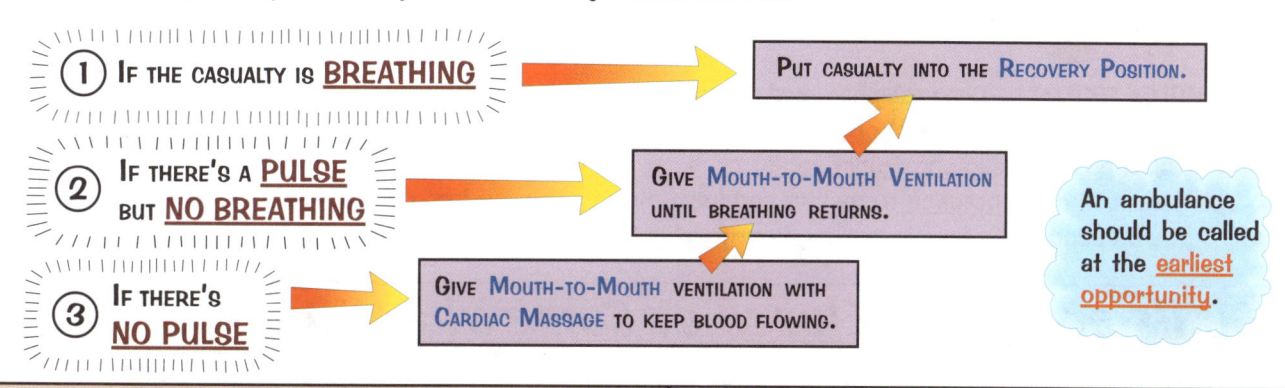

① IF THE CASUALTY IS **BREATHING** → PUT CASUALTY INTO THE RECOVERY POSITION.

② IF THERE'S A **PULSE** BUT **NO BREATHING** → GIVE MOUTH-TO-MOUTH VENTILATION UNTIL BREATHING RETURNS.

③ IF THERE'S **NO PULSE** → GIVE MOUTH-TO-MOUTH VENTILATION WITH CARDIAC MASSAGE TO KEEP BLOOD FLOWING.

An ambulance should be called at the earliest opportunity.

Mouth-to-Mouth Ventilation
The idea of mouth-to-mouth ventilation is for you to breathe for the casualty, forcing oxygen from your lungs into theirs:
1) Tilt the casualty's head back, open their mouth and pinch their nose closed.
2) Breathe in deeply, then press your lips onto theirs and breathe out slowly, making sure their chest rises.
3) Take your mouth away and let their chest fall again.

Repeat these steps until breathing returns or help arrives.

Cardiac Massage
1) Do 2 breaths of mouth-to-mouth ventilation.
2) Press down on the chest 15 times, a bit faster than once a second.
3) Repeat this pattern — 2 breaths, 15 chest compressions.
4) Look for signs of improvement, e.g. skin colour returning. Check for a pulse every minute.

DON'T PRACTISE THIS ON SOMEONE WHO'S CONSCIOUS*

These two together are called cardiopulmonary resuscitation (or CPR).

Finally, place in the Recovery Position

Once they're breathing okay, you can put the casualty into the recovery position. In this position, the head is tilted so that the airway won't be blocked by the tongue or by vomit. You should be able to leave the person unconscious like this while you go for help.

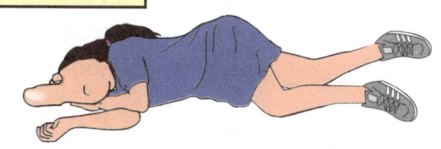

Easy as DR-ABC...
The ABC bit is the actual first aid, but you need to do the whole DRABC thing if you're the first to arrive at the scene. But remember you still need to get an ambulance as soon as you possibly can. And also — mouth-to-mouth is to restore breathing, cardiac massage is to keep blood flowing

*knock them out first

Section Three — Training and Sporting Skills

Skills

Skill is a word we use all the time. In PE, it's got a very fancy definition which you need to learn:

A SKILL is a learned ability to bring about the result you want, with maximum certainty and efficiency.

1) So the main point is that a skill is something you've got to learn. You can't be born with a skill, although you might learn it faster than other people.
2) With any skill, you always have a result in mind — you know what you want to do.
3) Skills should be performed with control and the minimum expense of energy/time.

Skills can be Basic or Complex

We say that particular actions which agree with the points above are skills, e.g. throwing a dart.

BASIC SKILLS — simple things like jumping or throwing:
1) You tend to master a lot of basic skills at an early age.
2) Basic skills tend to be transferable between many different activities. Just think of all the sports where you need a basic skill like running.
3) When learning a new sport or activity, it's really important that you've mastered all the basic skills first, before you attempt the more complex ones.

Jumping is a basic skill I can use in many situations.
So is this, though I prefer a lamp-post.

COMPLEX SKILLS — need a higher level of coordination and control:
1) Most complex skills are specific to one particular sport — like taking a football penalty kick (i.e. they're usually non-transferable).
2) They take more practice to master and have more scope for improvement — e.g. in tennis you'd spend more time improving your forehand than practising a basic skill like running.

Skills are Open, Closed or Somewhere In between

1) Skills (as with so much in PE) can be open or closed.
2) An open skill is one which is affected by many external factors, e.g. in golf, you can't just go up to the ball and take a swing, oblivious to what's going on around you. You need to consider things like the position of the hole, obstacles like trees, and the effect of the wind.

Wait!! Consider the external factors — like me!

3) A closed skill is one hardly affected by the environment or external factors, e.g. in darts, you usually make the same movements — you don't need to change them for different conditions.
4) To confuse the issue, most skills actually fall somewhere in between, e.g. taking a football penalty — your environment doesn't change much, but you can alter your movement to change the speed and aim of the shot. So it's partly closed and partly open.

Most gymnastic events like the beam involve performing many different closed skills.

5) You can compare the "openness" of skills by putting them on a continuous scale like this one:

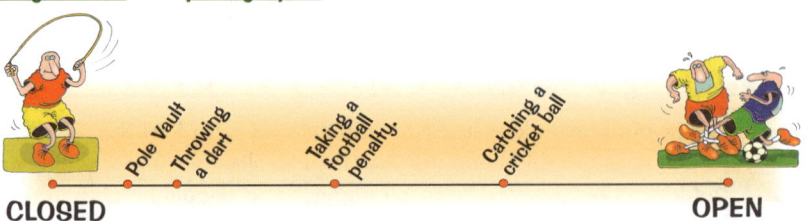

CLOSED — Pole Vault / Throwing a dart — Taking a football penalty — Catching a cricket ball — OPEN

Don't just sit there — get learning while there's skill time...

This whole open / closed lark is a bit weird. Basically — the more that doing a skill varies, and the more external factors matter, the more open a skill is. If you think pole vaulting is more open than throwing a dart — fine, as long as you can give reasons. In reality, it's pretty difficult to find any skills completely unaffected by any external factors — so most "closed" skills are actually a teeny bit open.

Section Three — Training and Sporting Skills

Skills

I know this page looks more like some dull IT module, but what it's <u>actually</u> about is the way your brain <u>works</u>, and how it <u>processes</u> information when you're <u>learning</u> a new skill.

The Brain Processes Information

This is the <u>basic</u> model of what your brain's up to when you're performing a skill (like when you're passing a football to someone else):

1) <u>INPUT</u> — this is <u>all</u> the information your brain receives. You <u>see</u> the position of the ball and the player you're aiming for. You <u>hear</u> players shouting. You <u>feel</u> the position of your feet and arms.

2) <u>DECISION MAKING</u> — this is where your brain <u>processes</u> the information and decides how to act.

3) <u>OUTPUT</u> — this is the actual <u>action</u> you carry out at the end, e.g. moving your leg to kick the ball.

4) <u>FEEDBACK</u> — the most important part of the <u>learning process</u>. Your brain looks at the result of the output and registers this information, so you'll know better next time. There are many ways of getting feedback:
   1) You can <u>feel</u> how well you kicked the ball — <u>intrinsic feedback</u>.
   2) You get verbal feedback from others, e.g. from a <u>coach</u> or <u>teacher</u> — <u>extrinsic feedback</u>.
   3) You can see how <u>successful</u> the performance was. Did the ball go where it was aimed? Did the intended player get it?

Memory and Perception

1) When your brain gets all the information (input), it has to <u>interpret</u> what it all means. This is called <u>perception</u>.
2) It filters out all the junk — <u>selective attention</u>.
3) The brain <u>searches</u> really quickly through all its stuff about sport — <u>memories</u> of similar situations.
4) And by thinking about the <u>past outcomes</u> stored in the memory, the brain can make an <u>informed decision</u> of how best to respond — I suppose that's what learning from experience is all about.

So here's an <u>extended</u> version of the basic diagram:

Selective Attention

1) The brain has a <u>limited channel capacity</u> — i.e. it can only process a certain amount of information at a time.
2) It has to <u>filter</u> out all the extra information it receives and only process the information relevant to performing the skill.
3) This is called <u>selective attention</u>.

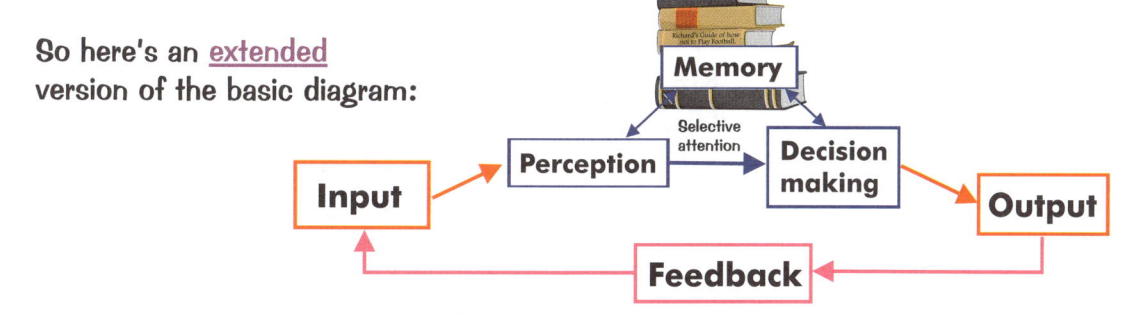

Information processing? Referee! — this isn't PE...

The flow diagrams are called <u>information processing models</u>. Yep, there's a lot of silly jargon to learn here. Practise drawing the diagrams and <u>scribbling down</u> what's happening at each stage. See what key words you missed and then try again. And keep trying till you've got it learnt.

Section Three — Training and Sporting Skills

Motivation and Mental Preparation

You've got to be physically fit to perform well at most sports — but it's just as important to be mentally fit. Attitude and motivation can really affect your performance. Here's how...

Motivation can be Intrinsic or Extrinsic

Motivation's about how keen you are to do something. It's what drives you on when things get difficult — your desire to succeed. You need to know about two kinds:

INTRINSIC MOTIVATION:
This comes from inside you. You play the sport because it's something you enjoy and would want to do well at — even if there were no prizes or rewards.

EXTRINSIC MOTIVATION:
This comes from outside. Maybe you want to do well because there's a big reward for succeeding — money or publicity, for example.

Cars, houses, jewellery, money, travel... It's mine — all mine.

Your Arousal Level shouldn't be Too High

Arousal is about being excited, keen and mentally ready (or unready) to perform a difficult task.

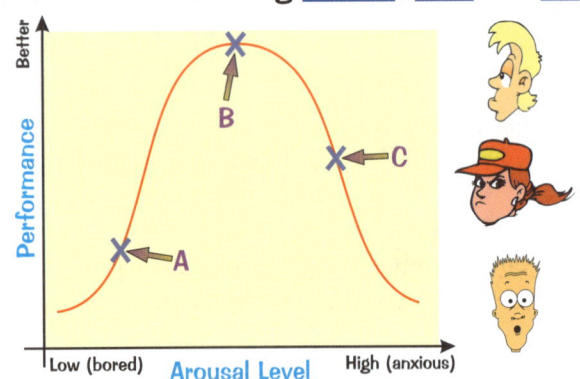

At A, the competitor isn't very excited — he's not very aroused — and so will probably not perform at his best.

At B, the competitor is determined and ready — her arousal level is just right — and this should mean that she performs well.

At C, the competitor is anxious and nervous — his arousal level is too high. He may become 'psyched out' or 'stressed out', and he won't be able to give his best performance.

This is the Inverted U Theory of arousal (since the graph looks like an upside-down letter 'U'). Too much or too little arousal stops you performing at your best — the best level is in the middle.

Goal Setting should be SMARTER

Goal setting means setting targets that you want to reach. Short-term goals that you can reach quite quickly are steps on the way to a long-term one — like winning an Olympic medal.

GOAL SETTING — helps training, because it:

1) Helps you get ready to perform, since you know what you want to achieve.

2) Helps you to feel in control, and so less anxious about a performance.

3) Gives you confidence when you reach a target.

4) Motivates you to work hard.

When you're setting goals, remember SMARTER.

S — SPECIFIC: Say exactly what you want to achieve.
M — MEASURABLE: So you can see if you've achieved it or not.
A — AGREED: You should agree the targets with your coach.
R — REALISTIC: Set goals you can realistically reach.
T — TIME-PHASED: So the long-term goal is reached in time.
E — EXCITING: Boring goals won't motivate you.
R — RECORDED: So that you can check your progress.

Inverted U — No, I like U as U are...

This page is pretty easy really. Remember the name 'Inverted U Theory' — that'll impress the examiners, which is always good. Then there's the handy SMARTER rule to help you with goal setting. Couldn't be simpler. But check regularly that you still know what SMARTER stands for.

Section Three — Training and Sporting Skills

Revision Summary for Section Three

Another section almost out of the way, and not a bad little one either. Not too long, and loads of juicy bits and blood and gore to keep you on your toes. Some of it could even be useful some day — when someone's unconscious, you'll be glad you worked your way through it... And if it helps in the Exam too — well, so much the better. All the more reason to learn it, that's what I say. So what are you waiting for... As always, keep going through them till you can answer every question without cheating.

1) Give three reasons why a warm-up is an important part of an exercise session, and two reasons why you should always do a cool-down.
2) Name four principles of training, and explain briefly what each one means.
3) Name four stages that a year's training can be broken into. What are the important features of each stage?
4) Name the four 'FITT' factors that must be decided when designing a training programme.
5) Name the three kinds of strength and three kinds of weight training. Describe the differences between the types of weight training, and their advantages and disadvantages.
6) Describe what is meant by: a) pressure training, b) circuit training, c) continuous training, d) Fartlek training, e) interval training. Give two advantages and two disadvantages of each of these methods.
7) Give three reasons why it's good to have a high aerobic fitness level. Describe the three main tests for aerobic fitness. How can you measure your heart rate?
8) Describe how you can test: a) endurance, b) strength, c) balance, d) agility, e) speed.
9) Describe these flexibility tests: a) the Shoulder Lift Test, b) the Sit and Reach Test.
10) What do you call an injury caused by: a) a sudden stress, b) a stress over a long period of time?
11) List some precautions you could take *before* an activity to help avoid injury. What precautions could you take during and after an activity?
12) Define soft tissue injuries and hard tissue injuries.
13) Injuries are divided into two types depending on whether you see blood. What are the two types called?
14) Explain exactly what these are: a) bruises, b) strains, c) sprains, and d) dislocations.
15) Why is the area around a fracture usually bruised?
16) What is a stress fracture? What causes it?
17) What are the symptoms of hypothermia and hyperthermia? How should you treat them? Which one's which? And why have they got so many letters?
18) What causes cramp, winding and stitch? How should you treat them?
19) How should you treat concussion?
20) What is shock, and how should you treat it?
21) What's the RICE method? What injuries can you treat with it? What injuries shouldn't you treat with it?
22) If you find someone unconscious, what are the first five things you should check?
23) How should you treat an unconscious casualty if they: a) are breathing, b) have a pulse but aren't breathing, c) don't have a pulse?
24) Describe how to give mouth-to-mouth ventilation and cardiac massage.
25) What position could you leave an unconscious casualty in while you go for help? (Give its name and describe it.) What are the benefits of this position?
26) Define a skill. What's the difference between a basic skill and a complex one?
27) What is an open skill? And a closed one?
28) Describe a model of how your brain processes information. Draw a quick sketch to illustrate it. What are the main stages in the model?
29) What is selective attention, and what are its advantages?
30) What's the difference between intrinsic and extrinsic motivation? Give examples of each.
31) Describe the Inverted U Theory of arousal.
32) Name seven principles of goal setting.

Section Three — Training and Sporting Skills

Section Four — Sport in Society

Leisure and Recreation

You get to do what you want in leisure time, instead of doing your chores and stuff — it's great. And people now have more leisure time than they did a while back — so it's even more important.

Leisure Time and Recreation

Most of our time is taken up by things that need to be done:
1) Social duties — going to school or work, and doing chores and things.
2) Bodily needs — mainly eating and sleeping.

In the time that's left, we can choose what we want to do. This is our leisure time.

Leisure is free time, when you're not meeting bodily or social needs.

Loads of people spend their leisure time doing some kind of recreation...

Recreation is something you do in your leisure time because you want to.

DIFFERENCES BETWEEN SPORT AND PHYSICAL RECREATION:

1) Sports are more competitive — they have rules, and the aim is always to win. Sports have organised events and competitions.

2) Physical recreation isn't as competitive — you're not competing against anyone but yourself, so you can set your own rules.

People Have More and More Leisure Time

LEISURE TIME IS INCREASING — people have loads more than they did fifty years ago due to:
1) Less time working — the working week is much shorter, and holidays are longer.
2) Retiring earlier — more people are taking early retirement.
3) More unemployment — largely due to jobs being taken over by machines.
4) Machines helping with household chores — e.g. washing machines, vacuum cleaners, dishwashers. They've gradually become better, cheaper and more widely available.

As people's leisure time increases, so does the demand for facilities and services to help fill that time. There's been huge growth in the 'leisure industry' in recent years — and it's likely to continue.

People are Influenced by the Attitudes of Others

Your family and friends can have a big influence on whether you do sport, and which sports you choose.

SUPPORT FROM FAMILY:
1) Parents can encourage their children to take up sports.
2) Some sports need special clothing or equipment. It's usually parents who fork out the cash.
3) Many children can't easily get to and from sporting activities. They often rely on their parents to get them there.

PEER PRESSURE:
1) Most people have a group of friends they spend most of their leisure time with. This group of friends is their peer group.
2) "The individual's behaviour and attitude can be affected by the group's behaviour and attitude." To say that in a less fancy way — "If all your mates play and like football, you'll probably play and like football."
3) "If a group's attitude towards sport is negative, then it's harder for individuals within the group to find opportunities to play sports." In a less fancy way — "If all your mates say that sport is rubbish and don't play it, you'll do less sport."

We're all individuals...

Memo to God re: creation — nice one!

Imagine you had no leisure time — you'd be at school all day. And after that, you'd have chores to do until it was time for bed. Things used to be like that (kind of), but now everyone has more leisure time. So you can use it all learning this page... and then work down pit... and lick road clean... and...

Participation in Sport

The decision about what sports to play is affected by many things, including the people around you.

Schools have a Big Role in Encouraging Sport

Your school can be just as important as your family and friends when it comes to sport:

1) Schools have a very big role to play in generating interest in sport — and if you enjoy sports at school you're more likely to take them up when you leave.
2) PE teachers can affect your attitude towards sport and PE. A good teacher can build up your confidence, identify your strengths and potential, make the activity enjoyable and provide coaching.
3) Schools introduce you to a wide range of different activities, teaching the basic skills which you can build on later. The National Curriculum sets out the minimum amount that all schools have to teach, but many schools will also offer examination courses, extra-curricular activities, proficiency testing and various other awards. Some PE might be taught as part of other subjects too — e.g. health awareness.
4) As well as actually taking part, there are numerous other sporting roles you might have the chance to adopt. These include official, observer, coach, captain, leader, organiser and choreographer.
5) A school might give you access to sports facilities you won't find elsewhere, as well as ICT equipment. They might also have sporting clubs and societies, and links with local sports clubs.

SPAMFACET — Other things affecting the Sports We Choose

S → SEX — It's hard for women to get involved in a lot of sports which people still consider 'male sports' — e.g. football, rugby, cricket.

P → POLITICS — Politics has a big effect on the availability of large-scale sporting and training facilities, and also on what sports are taught or played in schools. It can also make sports illegal.

A → AGE — Some sports are more popular with certain age groups. Most people aged 16-30 have loads of choice for sport, but more will choose to play tennis, say, rather than something like bowls. People over 50 are more limited physically in the sports they can choose — so they tend to do less strenuous activities like walking or swimming.

M → MONEY — Learning an activity like skiing isn't easy for most people in this country. Sports like this are more popular with wealthy people who can afford to go abroad to ski. Similarly many sports require expensive equipment which a lot of people couldn't afford.

F → FASHION — Sports or leisure activities can go in or out of fashion. In the 1980s, snooker and squash became very popular. In the 90s, aerobics became very fashionable with endless tedious celebrity fitness videos being released. Media coverage of sports can have a big effect on sporting fashions.

A → ACCEPTABILITY — Some sports are considered socially unacceptable by some people — e.g. they might object to off-road driving because of enviromental concerns, or horse racing because of cruelty to animals.

C → CHALLENGE/DANGER — Many people are attracted to sports with an element of risk, like climbing or motor racing. They wouldn't get the same stimulation and enjoyment from something like bowls.

E → ENVIRONMENT/CLIMATE/ACCESS — The area you live in affects the sports you choose — there's more opportunity for outdoor activities like hillwalking, rock-climbing or windsurfing in the Lake District than in the sprawling metropolis of Manchester.

T → TECHNOLOGY — Technology affects the availability, cost and safety of equipment, materials and facilities. It can also lead to improved teaching and training aids, which might encourage more participation.

If everyone takes part, there won't be any left...

Hmmm, schools. Just think — if it wasn't for schools, you wouldn't have to learn all about how schools encourage sport. The second half of the page shouldn't be too hard to learn — just so long as you can recall those key words. But do test yourself to make sure you really do know it.

Section Four — Sport in Society

Women in Sport

There used to be a lot of stupid and bigoted views that stopped female participation in sport — held by both men and women. We've come on a long way, but things still aren't equal.

Women used to be Discouraged from doing Sport

Compared to nowadays, people used to think very differently about women in sport — they thought that:
1) Physical activity was something to be done by men only and that it made women look very unattractive.
2) Women could harm themselves by doing too much physical activity.
3) Women should wear 'respectable' clothing that covered their bodies up (e.g. long dresses). This meant that playing sport was very uncomfortable.
4) Women should look after the home and the children — this meant they didn't have the time or energy to play sport.

Greta felt awfully uncomfortable in goal.

Attitudes to women in sport are much better today. More and more women are playing sport because they aren't being held back. Local authorities often have women-only evenings at gyms and swimming pools as an incentive for women to join in. They provide a relaxing environment for women to meet people with similar interests, while they get plenty of exercise at the same time.

Women's Sport tends to have a Lower Profile

Despite all this progress, women's sport still faces problems.
PROBLEMS FACING WOMEN'S SPORT:
1) Too many sports are still considered 'male only'.
2) Women are often not allowed to compete with men. This is even true in sports like snooker where factors like physical strength have no relevance. Showjumping is one of the few events where women can compete against men.
3) Poor media coverage — women's events usually have a lower profile than men's events.
4) Less sponsorship — companies want to sponsor the events with the most media attention — generally the men's events.
5) Less prize money — women's events usually have less prize money than men's events — even in sports where the women do get good media coverage.
6) Few role models for women — again, lack of media support is the main problem.

Sometimes men and women don't compete on a level playing field...

Women's Sport is now Promoted

WOMEN'S SPORTS FOUNDATION — set up in 1984 in the UK. It aims to:
1) Increase awareness of the issues surrounding women in sport.
2) Help girls and women to get involved in sport at all levels.
3) Encourage organisations to improve sporting opportunities for women.
4) Challenge inequality in sport and seek to bring about change.
5) Raise the profile of British sportswomen.

Promotion of women's sport — Doncaster Belles go up...

So as you can see, women really do get a rotten deal when it comes to sport. Remember — the stuff at the top of the page about attitudes towards women is what many people used to think, it's hopefully not how many people think today. There's lots of juicy points here — learn 'em.

Section Four — Sport in Society

Sporting Behaviour

The behaviour of both players and spectators has a big effect on any competition. You need to know about this behaviour, and how hooliganism eventually changed the way people watch football.

Etiquette — The Unwritten Rules

The rules of any sport are written down — but etiquette is like an unwritten code of behaviour.

ETIQUETTE IN SPORTS:

Etiquette in sport means fair play and good manners. It makes life better for everybody. For example:

1) Football players often kick the ball out of play if an opponent is injured — so they can be treated. At the throw-in, the team that kicked the ball out should be given the ball back.
2) At the end of a tennis match, players should shake their opponent's and the umpire's hand.

At the other end of the scale, gamesmanship (or 'psyching out' your opponent) is behaviour that's very close to cheating.

VIOLENCE BETWEEN PLAYERS:

1) Violence between competitors is rare in non-contact sports like athletics (where there's no direct aggression).
2) Fights do break out in aggressive team sports like rugby and ice hockey.
3) Some people say that violence among players causes spectator violence — but no one has proved or disproved this.
4) If a player has behaved violently, they can be fined or suspended (not allowed to play for a certain time) by the governing body — and their club can be fined.

It had all started out as a friendly game of dominoes.

Spectators have their Good Points and Bad Points

Having lots of spectators is an advantage for any club — but there is a downside.

THE UPSIDE OF SPECTATORS:

1) Crowds can influence a match — cheering on their team and putting off the opponents. This is one reason why playing at home is an advantage.
2) They buy tickets and other club merchandise (like shirts and scarves), which brings revenue (money) into a club.

SNAIL RACE — Hooliganism was a problem at the local snail races.

THE DOWNSIDE OF SPECTATORS:

1) Facilities are needed, and marshals have to be provided to supervise crowds.
2) The police may be needed to control large crowds — and clubs have to pay for this.
3) Hooliganism can be a problem.

Football Disasters Led to the Taylor Report

Hooliganism has caused disasters, so action had to be taken to try to solve the problem.

THE HEYSEL DISASTER
At the European Cup Final in 1985, 39 Juventus fans were killed when Liverpool supporters rushed towards them, making a wall collapse.

THE HILLSBOROUGH DISASTER
At the 1989 FA Cup semi-final 96 fans were crushed to death against fences round the pitch, after too many people had been let in to the stadium.

After these two disasters, the Taylor Report suggested ways to make stadiums safer:

RECOMMENDATIONS OF THE TAYLOR REPORT:

1) Stadiums had to have fences to separate opposing fans.
2) Stadiums in some divisions had to become 'all-seater' — there could be no more terraces full of people standing.
3) Club membership schemes were introduced, so known troublemakers could be barred from entering grounds.
4) Perimeter fences between crowds and the pitch were removed.
5) Closed circuit TV (CCTV) around stadiums now monitors fans.
6) Information is now shared by police forces in different countries.

Bad behaviour ruins sport — it's just not cricket...

There's a lot here. The Heysel and Hillsborough disasters, and the Taylor Report that followed were very important — so you should learn all about them. And, make sure you understand what etiquette is — and a couple of examples of it. Those are the main things — so away you go.

Section Four — Sport in Society

Local Sports Clubs

There are loads of rules to be followed and organising to be done if you want to play sport. Local sports clubs help their members with the boring stuff, so people can get on with playing.

Most Local Sports Clubs have a similar Structure

Local sports clubs often have a structure like the one below.

- **THE MEMBERS** — usually pay to join the club. They elect the committee.
- **COMMITTEE** — elected by the members to run the club.
- **CHAIRPERSON** — the top official who represents the club and chairs the meetings.
- **VICE-CHAIRPERSON** — takes over if the chairperson is away.
- **TREASURER** — manages the club's finances.
- **SECRETARY** — does all the boring jobs, like taking notes at meetings, and letting all the members know what's going on.
- **FIXTURES SECRETARY** — organises club events, both competitive (e.g. matches) and non-competitive (e.g. dinners).
- **MEMBERSHIP SECRETARY** — tries to enrol new members so the club can keep going.
- **COACH** — helps all club members to train, and coaches the club team.

Sports club committees — they're more interesting than toothache.

Local Sports Clubs are for the Members

LOCAL SPORTS CLUBS — deal with:
1) Administration — the paperwork and organisation needed to run the club.
2) Facilities — maintaining the playing, changing and social areas and equipment.
3) Competition — running competitions within the club, or against other clubs.
4) Coaching — helping its members improve their skills, and encouraging juniors to play.

Get out there and play.

There are three main types of Competition

A lot of sport's about competition, let's face it. These are the main ways competitions are organised:

1) **LEAGUE** — Each team or player plays against all the others at least once (often twice — home and away). They get points for winning or drawing a game. The winner is the player or team with the most points at the end of the season. Leagues are a very fair way to run a competition, because they reward consistency over a long time. The trouble is they may take too long, and if there are too many people or teams they may have to be divided up into smaller leagues.

2) **KNOCK-OUT** — It's played in rounds, with each player or team playing one game per round. They go through to the next round if they win, otherwise they're out of the competition. Knock-outs are easy to organise and quick to run, but they're not as fair as you only get one chance. On the other hand, they're more exciting to watch and take part in.

3) **LADDER** — The players are listed on a ladder. Each can challenge a player higher on the ladder, but only up to a certain number of rungs higher. If they beat them, they take their place on the ladder. This is no good for team sports and can be demoralising for new players who must start at the bottom.

League me alone — I don't want to learn all this...

Phew! There's some stuff on this page alright. That sports club structure is busy-as-a-bellyful-of-beans. The easiest way to get it stuck in your head is to fill in all the positions with real people from a real club. The rest of the page shouldn't be too hard — but just make sure you can recall it later.

Section Four — Sport in Society

Sporting Facilities

You might not need good facilities for most sports — but it definitely makes playing them easier. You've got to know about the differences between facilities, and the problems of planning them.

There are Indoor and Outdoor Sports Facilities

OUTDOOR FACILITIES — including pitches (e.g. for football, rugby, cricket), tracks (e.g. for athletics, motor racing, horse racing), facilities for water sports (e.g. outdoor swimming pool), and natural features (e.g. for cross-country running, canoeing).

INDOOR FACILITIES — usually purpose-built buildings such as swimming pools and sports halls (used for loads of sports, like tennis, basketball, badminton and football).

To Build Indoor Facilities You need to Plan ahead

These are some examples of questions that should be asked when planning an indoor facility.

1) Are people going to use it?
2) Can people park there?
3) Can it be used for other things?
4) Can people get to it?
5) What will it cost?
6) Is there any competition? (from similar facilities nearby)

Both the Public and Private Sectors Provide Facilities

PUBLIC SECTOR FACILITIES:
1) Owned by local authorities and councils.
2) Usually run at a loss (subsidised by taxes).
3) Examples include: sports pitches, leisure centres, swimming pools and sports halls.

PRIVATE SECTOR FACILITIES:
1) Owned by companies or individuals.
2) Run to make money or break even.
3) Examples include: sports stadiums (e.g. Wembley), tennis clubs, golf clubs, football stadiums and health clubs.
4) Include voluntarily run facilities, e.g. football, rugby and golf clubs, and things like church halls.

CENTRES OF EXCELLENCE:
Offer really good facilities for the best athletes:
1) Crystal Palace (athletics, swimming, and martial arts),
2) Bisham Abbey (tennis),
3) Lilleshall (football),
4) Holme Pierrepoint (water sports),
5) Plas-y-Brenin (outdoor activities),
6) National Cycling Centre.

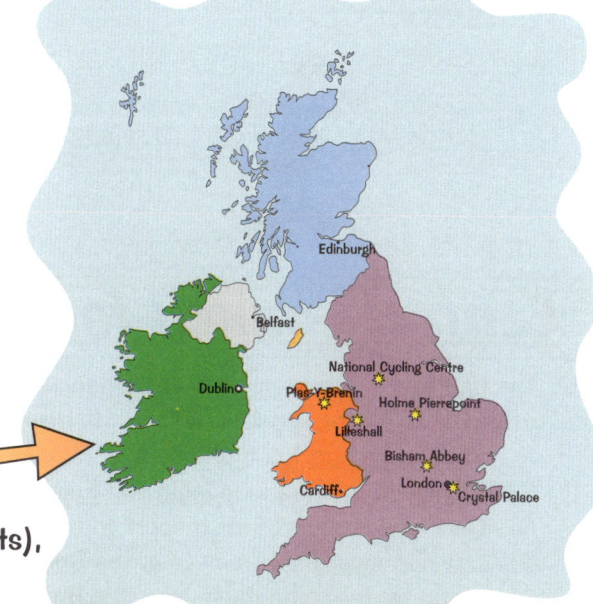

Map Showing the Centres of Excellence

Facilities, what can you say, hmmm yeah facilities, yep...

Most of this stuff is common sense and general knowledge. Learn the three main headings first — they should remind you of the rest of the stuff. Try and remember a couple of examples of private and public facilities in your local area — then you can just write about what they do.

Section Four — Sport in Society

Sporting Bodies and Organisations

Sporting bodies encourage and help people to play sport. There are loads and loads of them, all across the world. But don't worry — you only need to know about the ones on these two pages.

National Governing Bodies of Sport have Four Main Roles

GOVERNING BODIES — have four main roles:
1) To maintain the rules of the sport and keep discipline (e.g. by fining or banning competitors).
2) To promote the sport.
3) To organise international competitive events, and run the national team.
4) To organise national competitions.

Examples of the UK's sporting governing bodies are the FA (Football Association) and UKA (UK Athletics).

UK Sport — Used to be the Sports Council

In 1997 'UK Sport' was made from the old 'Sports Council'.
It was set up to produce top sporting performers in the UK.

UK SPORT — aims to:
1) Give the UK's world class performers excellent support.
2) Improve the UK's profile and influence on the international sporting stage.
3) Promote ethical behaviour and provide an anti-doping programme.
4) Persuade governing bodies that the UK is the best place to hold major sporting events and that UK Sport can run them.

Each Home Country has its own sports council too: Sports Council for Wales; Sports Council for Northern Ireland; Sport Scotland; Sport England.

HOME COUNTRY COUNCILS — aim to:
1) Increase participation in sports.
2) Improve the number and quality of facilities.
3) Increase sporting standards.
4) Allocate lottery funding.

Central Council for Physical Recreation — CCPR

The CCPR is a voluntary umbrella organisation for the governing bodies of all the different sports in Britain. It tries to:
1) Encourage sport and physical recreation.
2) Advise its members on legal and financial issues.
3) Give advice about British sport to other bodies and authorities.
4) Develop award schemes (e.g. the Sports Leader Awards, which is run by their charitable arm, the British Sports Trust).

CCPR — is funded by:
1) Donations from its members.
2) Sponsorship.
3) A grant from the UK Sports Council.
4) Sales of books, magazines and other things.

CCPR — resuscitation for the two-hearted...

There are three types of council to get to grips with — UK Sport, Home Country councils and the CCPR. Learn what they do and how they're different. It's not exciting, but it is important.

Section Four — Sport in Society

Sporting Bodies and Organisations

You've got to know about <u>all</u> these organisations, <u>and</u> what they <u>do</u>. It won't be as exciting as downhill skiing, but it beats the hell out of maths (allegedly). Get it learnt or chuck away marks.

International Olympic Committee — IOC

INTERNATIONAL OLYMPIC COMMITTEE (IOC):
1) Runs the Olympics.
2) Selects where the games are held.
3) Decides which sports are included.
4) Helps to plan the games.
5) Fights against doping and corruption in sport.

British Olympic Association — BOA

BRITISH OLYMPIC ASSOCIATION (BOA):
1) Organises the British Olympic team.
2) Raises money so the team can compete at the Olympics.
3) Works with governing bodies of sport to help the athletes prepare for the Olympics.
4) Coordinates British bids to host the Games.

National Coaching Foundation — NCF

NATIONAL COACHING FOUNDATION (NCF):
1) Works to improve the quality of coaching in the UK.
2) Helps the education and development of coaches.
3) Is concerned with all levels of coaching at all ages.

Shouting can Intimidate
coaching school

Sports Aid Foundation — SAF

SPORTS AID FOUNDATION (SAF):
1) Raises money to help athletes who can't afford to train or compete.
2) Gets money from National Lottery donations, sponsorship and grants.

Some days Wayne wished he could afford a bigger pole.

Countryside Commission — CC

COUNTRYSIDE COMMISSION (CC):
1) Looks after the countryside.
2) Advises authorities like the government on countryside issues.
3) Ensures the countryside is used for physical recreation.
4) Ensures the countryside is protected.
5) Set up the Country Code.

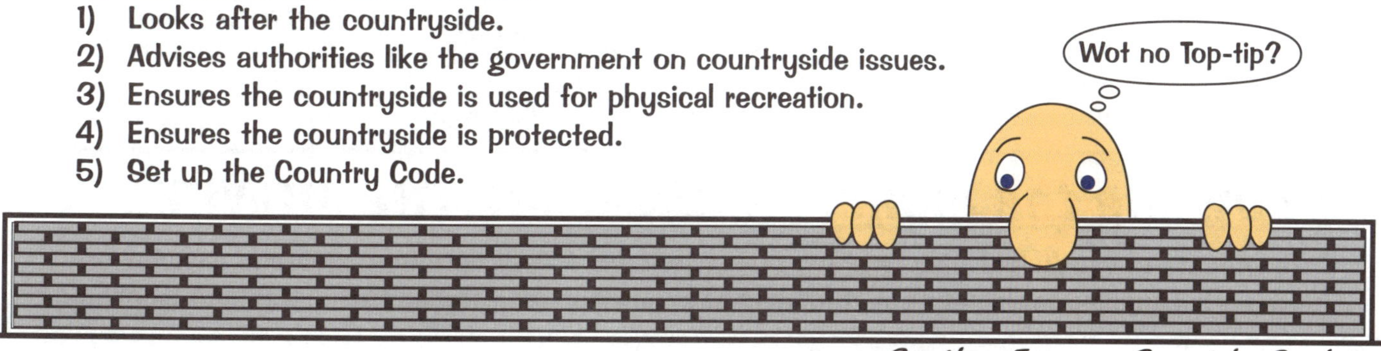

Wot no Top-tip?

Section Four — Sport in Society

Finance of Sport

You only have to look at what Manchester United's top player gets a week to see that there's a shed-load of money at the top end of sport. At the other end of the scale, the amateur players in "Dangleberry United" have to pay a club fee and match fee before they can play in the glorious Sunday League.

Amateur Sport is Run on Very Little

Funding for small clubs and recreational sports facilities comes from a variety of sources but money is generally very thin on the ground.

PUBLIC FACILITIES
Public sports facilities (e.g. public swimming pools) are subsidised by the local council to keep prices for the public low. Local councils get money for this from local taxes.

SMALL SPORTS CLUBS
Small sports clubs cover the costs of things like court hire and equipment with membership fees. Teams from these clubs pay match fees to cover the cost of entering the league. Gambling levies can also be a big source of income for voluntary clubs — e.g. from raffles.

PRIVATE FACILITIES
Private facilities often charge a lot to cover their cost and make a profit.

NATIONAL LOTTERY FUNDING
Groups can apply for lottery funding to build or improve sports facilities in an area. The competition for National Lottery funding is fierce and the applicants must have raised at least half the money themselves.

SPONSORSHIP
At the local level small businesses sponsor local teams. This generally involves buying the shirts and sticking their name on them.

Small Amateur Clubs & Recreational Sport

Professional Sport needs a Lot of Money

Popular sports and the people who play them at the top level can expect a load of money. But it ain't all big bucks and fast cars — less popular sports and their players must work hard to get the money they need.

TV AND RADIO
TV companies pay whooping amounts for the rights to show the biggest sporting events. The governing body of the sport involved gets that dosh. They use it to promote and develop their sport. Large companies get very excited and throw loads of sponsorship money at people and teams that get on the telly.

SPONSORSHIP AND MERCHANDISING
For big clubs and teams sponsorship means a heck of a lot more than a couple of shirts and a round of sandwiches. They can also rake in the money through sales of replica shirts and other such merchandise. It ain't as easy for people in lesser known sports like gymnastics where people have to pay their own way a lot of the time.

GRANTS
Up-and-coming sports stars can apply for funding from the Sports Aid Foundation (SAF) to cover the cost of their transport, training etc. The SAF gets money from donations and fund-raising. The British Olympic Association (BOA) covers the cost for the British Olympic team with money from fund-raising and commercial sponsorship. See page 51 for more on the SAF and BOA.

COMPETITIONS
Small scale competitions that don't command media attention have to rely on entrance fees to cover their costs. Larger events can cover costs through sponsorship — and an event like the Olympics can make a boat-full of money.

LARGE PROFESSIONAL CLUBS AND TOP CLASS SPORT

Show me the money — SHOW ME THE MONEY...

Lots and lots of words, but only nine key points to learn. Make sure you know the difference between the funding for big clubs and funding at a smaller level. Get all that and you're laughing.

Section Four — Sport in Society

Sponsorship

Sponsorship exists to give good <u>publicity</u> to the sponsors. Sponsorship funds sports, teams or individuals in part or in full. The more <u>famous</u> the sport, team or individual, the higher the payout.

Everything is Sponsored *from the Team to the Ball*

If people are going to <u>see</u> it, companies will slap their <u>name</u> on it, whether it's a person, team, league, stand, trophy, mascot, badge, or ball. This means big bucks for the <u>famous few</u>.

Free <u>transport</u> from MegaTravel Ltd

Free <u>accommodation</u> from Hotels R Us

Sports <u>scholarship</u> courtesy of Upman College

Free sports <u>equipment</u> from Dude Sports

Free <u>clothes</u> and <u>shoes</u> from the Cool Clothes Company

New <u>stand</u> paid for by Sugarfeine Energy Drink

<u>Event</u> and <u>league</u> paid for by Foley Computers

<u>Entrance fee</u>, <u>food</u> and <u>training</u> paid for by WheatyBeat Cereals

SPONSORSHIP CAN BE GOOD FOR SPORT — that's because it...
1) Pays for full-time sportspeople to <u>train</u> and <u>compete</u>.
2) Pays for <u>events</u> and <u>leagues</u>.
3) <u>Promotes</u> development of up-and-coming sportsmen and -women.

Sponsors *get a lot out of Sponsorship Too*

Why do sponsors give away all that dosh? Read on and learn their devious ways...

1) <u>FREE ADVERTISING</u> — See a good player using it and you'll want to use it.
2) <u>IMAGE</u> — The company becomes associated with winners.
3) <u>SCHOLARSHIPS</u> — Some universities and colleges offer places (at discounted grades) to students who excel at particular sports. In return universities gain prestige for sporting excellence.
4) <u>TAX AND HOSPITALITY</u> — Sponsors don't usually have to pay tax on the money they spend on sponsorship. They also get free tickets to the events they sponsor, which they can use to impress clients and employees.
5) <u>AREN'T THEY NICE</u> — Companies often sponsor charity and local events. Whether this is out of the kindness of their hearts or to improve their corporate image is by the by.

There is a *Negative* side to Sponsorship

It's not all 'fun in the sun' when it comes to sponsorship — this lot covers the bad bits.

I'm selling chickens to raise money for a new strip for the Cheltenham Ladies Tiddlywinks team.

1) Not <u>everyone</u> can get sponsorship — companies aren't interested in sponsoring people from sports which aren't <u>popular</u>.
2) It could all turn nasty — get <u>injured</u>, lose your <u>form</u> or get a <u>bad reputation</u> and it's bye-bye sponsorship deal.
3) Abuse of power — associating cigarettes and alcohol with sport gives a <u>false</u> image of health.

CGP CGP CGP CGP (CGP — Official Sponsors of page 53)...
Sponsorship is a good way of getting money into sport. On the surface, it looks like a win-win situation for everyone, but it does have downsides. Make sure you know <u>who</u> gets <u>what</u> out of it, and who gets <u>nowt</u>. And <u>memorise</u> all the ways that companies get their names into sport.

Section Four — Sport in Society

Sport and the Media

You <u>can't avoid sport</u> — it's there in the daily papers, on the radio, in books, in films, on the Internet. Choose any type of media and there it is. Which is great for me cos I love it.

Sport turns up Everywhere from Papers to the Internet

1) <u>TV</u> and <u>Radio</u>  
2) <u>Cable</u> and <u>Satellite</u> — pay-per-view events 
3) <u>Ceefax</u> and <u>Teletext</u> 
4) <u>Internet</u> 
5) <u>Newspapers</u> and <u>Magazines</u> 
6) <u>Books</u> and <u>Films</u>

SPORTS PROGRAMMES: Live sport, highlights, quiz shows, documentaries, news.

SPORTS ARTICLES: Sports results/predictions, behind the scenes, players' private lives, biographies.

The media coverage of sport relies heavily on <u>technology</u>. Apart from making all these forms of coverage possible, it also improves them with things like <u>instant replays</u>, <u>photo finishes</u>, <u>underwater cameras</u>, <u>split times</u>, and timing to hundredths or <u>thousandths of seconds</u>.

The Media has a Good Effect on Sport...

The coverage of sport in the media does good stuff for sport.

<u>Money</u> — Media companies pay for the rights to show a sport — <u>sponsorship</u> for a sport will also <u>increase dramatically</u> if it's popularised by the media.

<u>Education</u> — People learn about the <u>rules and tactics</u> of sports.

<u>David Beckham</u> — (OK I couldn't think of a good 'D'). Produces <u>role models</u> for people to aspire to. If the role models stay good, everything's fine and dandy.

<u>Inspiration</u> — Brings sport to people who may not experience it otherwise. This can <u>encourage participation</u>.

<u>Aid to Coaching</u> — Sport on TV and video lets you <u>study the performance</u> of others.

Referee! You've got to be kidding!

The media: bringing sport & inspiration.

...and a Bad Effect on Sport

The media does lots of good for sport, but it has a <u>dark side</u> to it tooooooo....(that was supposed to sound eerie).

<u>Bias</u> — Only the really popular spectator sports get plenty of coverage. Very <u>little coverage</u> is given to <u>less popular sports</u>, starving them of all the benefits shown above.

<u>Lack of attendance</u> — Watching it live on telly means you're not at the game — <u>reducing ticket sales</u>, then the media 'steals' more of this money with 'Pay-per-view' or channel subscription fees.

<u>Overload</u> — "SPORT, SPORT, SPORT! It's all that's on" — <u>too much sport</u>. (According to mum).

<u>Open season</u> — <u>Sports stars are hounded</u> by the media, who are quick to pounce if a sports superstar's halo slips.

<u>Demands</u> to comply — The media actually <u>imposes</u> rules on sports to make them <u>more exciting</u>, e.g. tie breaks were introduced into tennis as a result of <u>media pressure</u>.

The sinister face of the media

The only sport on the Net I ever hear about is surfing...

Like with sponsorship, the media's involvement in sport isn't just a bed of roses. Learn what things sport <u>relies</u> on the media for, but know how it <u>suffers</u> from media coverage as well.

Section Four — Sport in Society

Amateurs and Professionals

It's dead important to know the difference between an amateur and a professional. It's all about money — professionals get paid but amateurs don't. All the info you need to learn is here.

Pros do it for Money — Amateurs for Love

You've got to know what the difference between an amateur and a professional is. It's easy.

AMATEURS — don't get paid for playing sport — they do it as a hobby because they like it.

PROFESSIONALS — get paid for playing their sport — it's their full-time job.

I play hockey because I love it.
I play golf for £2million a year.

1) Some sports are totally amateur, e.g. hockey.
2) Others have professionals and amateurs who compete separately, e.g. football.
3) Others are open — everyone competes against everyone else, e.g. tennis.

Pros and Ams — It was all a Matter of Class

The class system had a lot to do with how sport was divided into amateurs and professionals.

Amateurs were gentlemen — from the wealthy upper classes. They could afford to play just for fun.

Professionals were from a lower class. They competed for money, often just doing things for a bet.

Sport's attitude towards professionals has changed over the years.

1) The Olympics were only supposed to be for amateurs — that was the original rule.
2) But people started to bend the rules — they got paid, but competed as amateurs so they could take part in the Olympics.
3) It was becoming impossible to decide who was a true amateur, so the word 'amateur' was dropped from the Olympic rule book.
4) Governing bodies and the IOC (International Olympic Committee) now decide who can compete in the Olympics.

1) The Amateur Athletic Association started up in 1880. No professionals could join.
2) Professional football became legal in 1884.
3) Rugby split into two codes in 1895 — Rugby League players could be paid, but Rugby Union players couldn't.
4) Money from TV companies and sponsorship means that professional athletes can now earn £millions a year.

Most sports didn't let amateurs and professionals compete together — but cricket did.
Amateurs were 'gentlemen', and professionals 'players'. They usually played on the same team — but once a year they played against each other in the 'Gentlemen and Players' match.

People thought sport and money didn't mix — gambling on most sports was banned to discourage cheating.

Shamateurs — The Paid Amateurs

Amateur athletes wanted to find ways to train full-time, without being classed as professionals.

SCHOLARSHIPS — Colleges offer talented people the chance to train full-time for free — without doing much actual studying.

TRUST FUNDS — Prize money is paid into a trust fund. Athletes can take living expenses from the fund during their career — and get the rest when they retire.

SPONSORSHIP — e.g. athletes get paid for wearing a company's logo on their clothing.

'EXPENSES' PAYMENTS — These are often much more than what the athletes actually spend.

TOKEN 'JOBS' — Talented athletes can be given 'jobs' where they don't have to do anything, so they can train full-time.

GIFTS — Things like cars could be given as presents, and then sold.

ILLEGAL PAYMENTS — Nothing fancy here. Just take the cash and keep quiet.

Some companies will pay a fortune to have their logo on a sportsperson's clothing.

I amateur-rifically wealthy competitor...not!

There's a lot of information on this page — it's pretty dull, but hopefully not too bad. Make sure you know the stuff about the Olympics and cricket — it's dead important. The last section's also closely linked to the Olympics — and could easily be in an Olympic Games question in the exam.

Section Four — Sport in Society

International Sport

International competitions were first organised in the 19th century — and since then they've just got bigger and bigger. Learn about their pros and cons, and how attitudes towards them vary.

There are Loads of International Sporting Events

There are loads of international competitions. You should know a bit about some important ones...

- **THE OLYMPIC GAMES:** Summer and winter competitions held every four years.
- **THE PAN-AMERICAN GAMES:** Held every four years for countries in North, South or Central America.
- **THE COMMONWEALTH GAMES:** Held every four years and open to countries in the Commonwealth (the group of countries that used to be in the British Empire).
- **WORLD CUPS:** In cricket, rugby, football — all held every four years.

Nowadays, nearly every major sport has its own world championships.

Big International Competitions have Pros and Cons

These big tournaments all have their good points — but they can also cause problems.

ADVANTAGES
1) Players and supporters from different countries can meet, and experience different cultures and ways of life.
2) Competition between the best athletes in the world constantly pushes standards higher.
3) International events encourage people from all around the world to take part in sport.

DISADVANTAGES
1) Big tournaments are expensive to organise, so poor countries can't afford to stage them.
2) Not even rich countries are willing to host big competitions without help from big business — and this makes sport more commercialised.
3) Some countries want success at sport to 'prove' they are more successful than an enemy. The USA and USSR used to do this.

This high jump competition is sponsored by COMFI-PILLOWS

Different Countries have Different Attitudes to Sport

Every country wants success in sport — it gives status and pride, can bring a nation together and make people healthier. But different countries promote sport in different ways...

UNITED KINGDOM
1) PE is compulsory in schools.
2) Grants and sponsorship are available for promising talent.
3) Some top competitors have trust funds.
4) 'Sport for All' campaigns boost participation.

USA
1) PE is compulsory in schools.
2) School and college sport is high profile and attracts big sponsorship.
3) Scholarship schemes help promising athletes.
4) Top college athletes are drafted into professional leagues.

FORMER EASTERN BLOC
(The countries that were dominated by the USSR.)
1) Sport was controlled by the state.
2) Talented children were trained from a very young age — and then given token jobs in the army or industry.
3) Sport has been more open since 1989.

THIRD WORLD COUNTRIES
1) Popular sport has to be cheap — football and athletics are booming.
2) International success will earn money.
3) Top athletes are often given token government jobs.

Event-ually you'll have to learn this well...

There's quite a lot here again. You won't really need to know much about individual competitions — just as long as you know they exist and can name a few of them. The most important bits are the pros and cons of hosting a major sporting event — so spend a bit more time on these.

Section Four — Sport in Society

The Olympic Games

The Modern Olympic Games have been around since 1896 — and they've changed quite a bit since then. You need to know a bit about the history of the games, and the pros and cons of playing host.

Being a Host City has its Good and Bad Points

The Olympics are always hosted by a city, not a whole country. Hosting the Games should bring only advantages — but it doesn't always work out like that...

ADVANTAGES
1) The host city gets added prestige — useful if you want to attract trade and tourism.
2) The facilities built for the Games can be used by the locals after the events have finished.
3) Businesses in the host city will do masses of extra trade during the Games.
4) The organisers can try to make a profit.

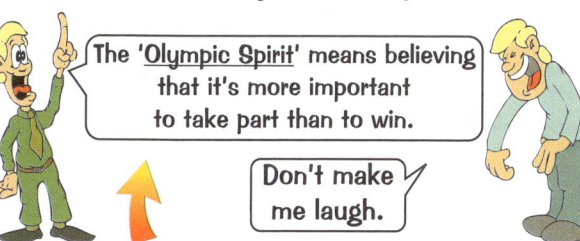

The 'Olympic Spirit' means believing that it's more important to take part than to win.

Don't make me laugh.

(This is what the organisers intended, anyway.)

The first ever Olympic Games were held in 776 BC in Ancient Greece.

Sponsored by Acropolis & Co.

DISADVANTAGES
1) It's getting more expensive to host the Games every time.
2) If there are problems, the organisers could lose enormous amounts of money.
3) Security could be a problem — hooligans or terrorists might disrupt the Games.
4) If a city's infrastructure (e.g. its phone or transport systems) can't cope, it could lead to frustration for locals and visitors.

The Olympic Games have had Their Ups and Downs

Since the Modern Olympics started in 1896, there have been quite a few ups and downs.

1896 in ATHENS — The first Modern Olympic Games were organised by Baron de Coubertin. Only men could compete. (See page 46.)

1936 in BERLIN — Hitler wanted the Games to prove the superiority of white northern Europeans. He stormed out of the stadium when the black American, Jesse Owens, won four gold medals.

1972 in MUNICH — Palestinian terrorists kidnapped nine Israeli athletes. The hostages, five terrorists and a policeman were killed after a rescue attempt failed.

1980 in MOSCOW — The USA and many other countries boycotted the Games (i.e. they didn't go to them) as a protest against the Soviet invasion of Afghanistan.

1984 in LOS ANGELES — The Games made a big profit, but were thought to be too commercial — nearly everything was sponsored by multinational companies. The USSR boycotted these Games in retaliation for the American boycott in 1980.

1992 in BARCELONA — No boycotts, and South Africa entered a team for the first time since 1964, when it was banned because of its racist apartheid laws.

The Olympic Games — a torch of class...

The history of the Olympics is important. You might be asked whether you think the 'Olympic Spirit' is still the same as it was originally — you'll need to back up your opinion with facts. Don't worry, the pros and cons above are similar to those on page 56 about international competitions.

Section Four — Sport in Society

Revision Summary for Section Four

Well, that's your lot — the final section out of the way. All you have to do now is to make sure you know it all. There are quite a lot of questions here — but like before I wouldn't try to do them all at once. Just take it easy at first, and you'll be storming through the lot in no time. Enjoy...

1) What's the difference between leisure time and recreation?
2) Give examples of some physical, mental and social benefits of physical recreation.
3) What's the difference between sport and physical recreation?
4) Give four reasons why people generally have more leisure time now than they did 50 years ago.
5) Give three examples of how somebody's family can affect their participation in sport.
6) What is peer pressure? How can it influence somebody's participation in sport?
7) Explain how schools can have an important influence on people's attitudes towards sport.
8) Name nine factors that can affect which sports someone takes part in.
9) Describe the structure of a local sports club.
10) Describe 3 ways competitions can be organised, and give advantages and disadvantages for each.
11) Give four reasons why women used to be discouraged from participating in sport.
12) What problems does women's sport still face today? How does the Women's Sports Foundation aim to help solve these problems?
13) What is etiquette? Give two examples of etiquette in sport. What is gamesmanship?
14) Give two ways spectators can help a sports club. What disadvantages could there be in allowing spectators to watch a sporting event?
15) Describe six recommendations made by the Taylor Report after the Heysel and Hillsborough disasters.
16) Describe four main roles of a national sporting governing body.
17) Draw a diagram to show the structure of a typical local sports club. What are the duties of the chairperson, vice-chairperson, treasurer, secretary, fixtures secretary and membership secretary?
18) Give four functions of a local sports club.
19) Give two examples of outdoor sporting facilities and two examples of indoor facilities.
20) What kinds of things should be considered when planning a new sporting facility?
21) Describe the main differences between public sports facilities and private sports facilities.
22) What are the centres of excellence? Give a couple of examples.
23) Give four aims of UK Sport, four sporting aims of the Home Country Councils, and four aims of the CCPR. How is the CCPR funded?
24) Describe the roles of the IOC, the BOA, the NCF, the SAF and the CC. And what do all those initials stand for?
25) Give five possible sources of funding for small clubs and recreational sports facilities.
26) Give two big sources of funding for important clubs playing popular sports.
27) How can companies benefit from sponsoring sports events or individual competitors? Give three examples of the negative side of sponsorship.
28) Describe five positive and five negative effects that the media can have on sport.
29) What's the difference between an amateur and a professional? How did this difference come about?
30) Describe seven ways a competitor could get paid for competing but remain classed as an amateur.
31) Give four examples of big international sporting events. Describe three benefits and three disadvantages of big international sporting competitions.
32) Describe very briefly the different attitudes to sport in: a) the UK, b) the USA, c) the former Eastern Bloc, and d) the Third World.
33) Give four benefits and four drawbacks to hosting the Olympic Games.
34) When were the first Modern Olympics held? Who organised them? Describe the events which blemished the Games in: a) Berlin in 1936, b) Munich in 1972, and c) Moscow in 1980.

Section Four — Sport in Society

Index

A
AAA (Amateur Athletics Association) 55
ABC first aid treatment 39
abdomen 38
abduction 3
acceptability of sports 45
access to facilities 45
active stretches 21
acute injuries 36
adduction 3
adipose tissue 18
administration 48
adrenaline 14
aerobic fitness testing 34
aerobic system 19
aerobic training 15
age 22
aggression 24, 47
agility 12, 28
agility testing 35
airway 39
alcohol 11, 12, 26, 27
allergies 28
altitude training 28, 31
alveoli 6
Amateur Athletics Association 55
amateurs 52, 55
ambulance 39
amino acids 16
anabolic agents (steroids) 26
anaemia 16, 28
anaerobic system 19
anaerobic training 15
analgesics, narcotic 26
angina 9
anorexia 18
antagonistic muscles 5
anti-doping programme 50
anxiety 11, 28, 42
apartheid 57
arousal 42
arteries 9, 15
arterioles 14
articles on sport 54
asthma 28
Athens Olympics 57
athlete's foot 25
attention 41
attitude 42, 45

B
backbone 2
balance 12, 16, 28
balance test 35
ball and socket joint 3
Barcelona Olympics 57
Baron de Coubertin 57
basal metabolic rate 18
basic skill 40
B CALM 27
Beckham, David 54
behaviour 45
benefits of exercise 13
Berlin Olympics 57
beta blockers 27
Bisham Abbey 49
blisters 25, 37
blood cells 9, 15
blood doping 27
blood flow 30
blood plasma 9
blood vessels 9, 37
BMR (basal metabolic rate) 18
BOA (British Olympic Association) 51
body composition 12, 18
body fat 15
body temperature 8, 38
bone 37
bone fracture 37
bones 1, 15
boycott 57
brain 41
breathing 15, 39
British Olympic Association 51
British Sports Trust 50
bronchi 6
bronchioles 6
bruising 37, 38
bunions 25

C
calcium 16
calf muscle 37
calories 16
capillaries 9, 15
carbohydrates 16
carbohydrate loading 17
carbon dioxide 6, 14
cardiac massage 39
cardiac muscles 4
cardiac output 8
cardiopulmonary resuscitation 39
cardiovascular endurance 12, 19
carotid artery 34
carotid pulse 34
cartilage 1, 2, 15, 37
cartilaginous joints 2
CC (Countryside Commission) 51
CCPR (Central Council for Physical Recreation) 50
CCTV (closed circuit TV) 47
Central Council for Physical Recreation 50
centres of excellence 49
chafing 37
chairperson 48
challenge 45
channel capacity 41
characteristics, inherited 20
charity events 53
cheering 47
chest 39
chin 35
chronic injury 36
circuit training 33
circulation 15, 39
circulatory system 15
class system 55
climate 28, 45
closed circuit TV 47
closed fracture 37
closed injury 37
closed skill 40
clothing 36
club structure 48
coach 48
coaching 54
coccyx 2
code of behaviour 47
college sport 56
colliding 36
combination testing 35
commercialism 56, 57
committees 48
Commonwealth Games 56
competition 31
competitions 52
complex skill 40
compression 38
concussion 36, 38
condition, physical 13
condyloid joint 3
confidence 42
confusion 15
connective tissue 2
constipation 26
continuous training 33
contraction 5
control 40
cool-down 30, 36
coordination 12, 28, 40
corns 25
corticosteroids 27
Coubertin, Baron de 57
councils 49
Countryside Commission 51
coverage of sport 54
CPR (cardiopulmonary resuscitation) 39
cramp 5, 38
cross training 31
Crystal Palace 49
cuts 37
CV (cardiovascular) endurance 12, 19

D
danger 45
Dangleberry United 52
Dark Side 54
David Beckham 54
decision making 41
dehydration 17, 38
deoxygenated blood 8
determination 24
diaphragm 38
diastolic pressure 8
diet 11, 12, 16, 17
dietary fibre 17
digestive system 17
direct aggression 24
disabilities 12
dislocations 37
diuretics 26
doping 26
doping, blood 27
DRABC first aid treatment 39
draft 56
drugs 11, 12, 26
dynamic strength 20

E
Eastern Bloc 56
ectomorphs 23
efficiency 40
elbow, tennis / golfer's 36
elections 48
elevation 38
emotional health 11
endomorphs 23
endurance 13, 19, 33
endurance, cardiovascular 12
endurance, muscular 12, 19
endurance testing 35
endurance training 15
energy 18
environment 11, 28, 36, 40, 45
enzymes 16
equipment 36
ethical standards 50
etiquette 47
exercise 13, 14
exercise, aerobic 15
experience 22, 28
expiration (breathing out) 7
explosive strength 12, 20
extension 3
external factors 40
extrinsic feedback 41
extrinsic motivation 42
extroverted 24

F
facilities 57
falling 36
fartlek training 33
fashion 45
fast twitch muscle fibres 4
fats 16
fatigue 28
fatty acids 16
feedback 41
femur 1
fibrous joints 2
fights 47
finance 52
fitness 12
FITT 31
flexibility 21, 22, 35
flexion 3
flip-flops 25
football disasters 47
footwear 36
fractures 36, 37
freely movable joints 2
funding 52

G
gambling levies 52
gamesmanship 47
gaseous exchange 6
gender 22
general fitness 12
Gentlemen and Players 55
gliding joint 3
glucose 16, 19
glycogen 14, 16
goal setting 42
goals, long-term 13, 42
goitre 16
golfer's elbow 36
governing bodies 48
grants 52, 56
grazes 37

H
haemoglobin 6, 16
hamstring 37
hard tissue injury 37
Hart, Tony 23
Harvard step test 34
hay fever 28
health 11
heart 15, 38
heart attacks 9
heart rate 14, 34
height 12
Heysel disaster 47
Hillsborough disaster 47
hinge joint 3
HIP DAD 12
Hitler 57
Holme Pierrepoint 49
Home Country councils 50
hooliganism 47, 57
hormones, adrenaline 14
hormones, peptide 26
hygiene 11, 25
hygiene routine 25
hypertrophy 15
hyperthermia 38
hypothermia 38

I
ice 38
illness 12, 28
illness, mental 18
image 53
immovable joints 2
indirect aggression 24
indoor sports facilities 49
inequality 46
inflammation 25, 36
information 41
informed decisions 41
infrastructure 57
inherited characteristics 20
injuries 11, 12, 21, 22, 36
input 41
inspiration 54
inspiration (breathing in) 7
interest in sport 45
internal feedback 41
international competitions 48, 56
International Olympic Committee 51, 55
Internet 54
interval training 33
intrinsic feedback 41
intrinsic motivation 42
introverted 24
Inverted U Theory 42
involuntary muscles 4
IOC (International Olympic Committee) 51, 55
iodine 16
iron 16
isometric contraction 5
isometric training 32
isotonic contraction 5
isotonic training 32
isovindaloo training 32

J
Jesse Owens 57
joint injuries 37
joints 1, 3, 15

K
kidneys 17
kilocalories 18
kilojoules 18
knock-out competitions 48

Index

L

lactic acid 14, 19, 30
ladder competitions 48
league competitions 48
learning process 41
leisure time 44
lifestyle 11
ligaments 2, 15, 37
Lilleshall 49
limited channel capacity 41
liver 16
local anaesthetics 27
local authorities 49
local councils 52
local sports clubs 48
logo 55
long-distance runners 4
long-term goals 13, 42
Los Angeles Olympics 57
lottery funding 50

M

major sporting events 50
marijuana 27
marrow, bone 1
marshals 47
maximal oxygen consumption 34
media 54
media attention 52
membership secretary 48
memory 41
menstrual cycle 22
menstruation 28
mental benefits of exercise 13
mental illness 18
mental preparation 28, 42
merchandise 47
mesomorphs 23
minerals 16
mobility 21
Modern Olympic Games 57
money 42, 54
Moscow Olympics 57
motivation 42
mouth-to-mouth ventilation 39
movement time 20
multinational companies 57
multistage fitness test 34
Munich Olympics 57
muscle 4, 5, 37, 38
muscle atrophy 5
muscle contraction 5
muscle fatigue 5
muscle pull 37
muscle repair 14
muscle strength 32
muscle tear 37
muscle tone 32
muscular endurance 12, 19

N

narcotic analgesics 26
National Coaching Foundation 51
national competitions 48
National Cycling Centre 49
national governing bodies 48
National Lottery 52
NCF (National Coaching Foundation) 51
nerve impulses 4
nervousness 42
nervous system 4
night vision 16
non-transferable skills 40
nutrients 17
nutrition 16

O

obesity 18
officials 36
oil 16
Olympic Games 55, 56
open tournaments 55
open fracture 37
open injury 37
open skill 40
opportunities for women 46
organisations 50
ossification 1
out-of-season training 31
outdoor sports facilities 49
output 41
over-exercising 38
overload 30, 32, 33
overstretching 37
Owens, Jesse 57
oxygen 6, 14
oxygen capacity 22
oxygen debt 14, 30
oxygenated blood 8

P

Pan-American Games 56
participation 45, 54
passive stretches 21
patterns of exercise 33
pay-per-view 54
peaking 31
peer groups 45
peer pressure 45
penalties 40
peptide hormones 26
perception 41
performance 28, 42
performance-enhancing drugs 26
perimeter fences 47
periosteum 1
personal hygiene 11
personality 24
PE teachers 45
physical benefits of exercise 13
physical condition 13
physical manipulation 27
physical recreation 44
physiological factors 28
pivot joints 3
Plas-Y-Brenin 49
plasma, blood 9
platelets 9
PLEASED 11
police 47
politics 45
posture 13, 21
power 20
practice 40
pre-season preparation 31
pressure training 32
prevention of injuries 36
principles of training 30
private facilities 49, 52
prizes 42
process 41
professional sport 52, 55
profits 57
programmes 54
promotion of sport 52
proteins 16
psyched out 42
psychological factors 12
public facilities 49
publicity 42, 53
pulled muscle 36
pulmonary circuit 8
pulse 38, 39
punishments 27

R

radial artery 34
reaction time 20, 22
reactions 12
recovery position 38, 39
recovery time 14
recreation 44
recuperation 31
red blood cells 9, 15
referees 36
relaxation 28
relaxation of muscles 5
repair of muscles 14
respiratory system 6, 15
rest 36, 38
resuscitation 39
rewards 42
RICE method 38
rickets 16
role of schools 45
rotation 3
Rugby League 55
Rugby Union 55
rules 36

S

4 S's 12
sacrum 2
SAF (Sports Aid Foundation) 51, 52
safety 11
salt 38
scholarships 53, 55, 56
scurvy 16
security 57
selective attention 41
serious injuries 39
sex 22, 45, 46
shin splints 36, 37
shock 38
shoulder lift test 35
shunting 14
sit and reach test 35
skeleton 1
skill 40, 41
skin 37
sleep, lack of 28
slightly movable joints 2
slow twitch muscle fibres 4, 19
SMARTER 42
smoking 12, 26
social benefits of exercise 13
social duties 44
soft tissue injury 37
somatotypes 12, 23
South Africa 57
specific fitness 12
spectators 47
speed 12, 20
speed testing 35
sphygmomanometer 8
sponsorship 52, 53, 55, 56
SPOR 30
Sport for All 56
sporting behaviour 47
sporting bodies 50
sporting injuries 36
sporting organisations 51
Sports Aid Foundation 51
sports clubs 52
sports facilities 49
Sports Leaders Awards 50
sports stars 54
sprains 37, 38
sprinters 4
staleness 28
stamina 12
static strength 20
step-ups 34
steroids, anabolic 26
stimulants 26
stitch 38
stores of glycogen 14
stork stand test 35
strain 37, 38
strength 12
strength, dynamic 20, 32
strength, explosive 12, 20, 32
strength, static 20, 32
strength testing 35
strength training 15
stress 11, 13, 36, 42
stress fractures 37
stretching 21, 30, 38
stroke volume 8, 15
strokes 9
sugars 16
suppleness 12, 21
sweat 25
sweating 14
swellings 37, 38
synergists (muscles) 5
synovial joints 2
systemic circuit 8
systolic pressure 8

T

targets 42
target zone 19
Taylor Report 47
teamwork 13
tear, of muscle 37
technique 36
technology 28, 45, 54
tendons 1, 2, 36, 37
tennis elbow 36
tension 13
terraces 47
terrorists 57
Third World 56
thyroid 16
time-phased 42
timing 12
tissues, body 37
tobacco 26
tongue 39
Tony Hart 23
tourism 57
trace elements 16
trachea 6
training, aerobic 15
training, anaerobic 15
training duration 30
training, endurance 15
training frequency 30, 31
training intensity 30, 31
training methods 32
training programmes 31
training routines 30
training sessions 30, 31
training, strength 15
training times 31
training types 31
transferable skills 40
treasurer 48
trust funds 55, 56
12-minute run 34
twisting 37

U

UK Sport 50
unconsciousness 38, 39
urine 17
urine testing 27

V

vasoconstriction 14
vasodilation 14
veins 9
verbal feedback 41
verrucas 25
vertebrae 2
vice-chairperson 48
violence 47
vital capacity 15
vitamins 16
VO_2 7
VO_2 Max 7, 15, 19, 34
voluntary muscles 4
vomit 39

W

warm-down 30
warm-up 30, 36
warm weather training 31
water 17
weather 21, 28
weight 12
weight training 32
well-being 11
white blood cells 9
WHO (World Health Organisation) 11
winding 38
women in sport 46
Women's Sports Council 46
World Health Organisation 11